I CHOSE THE SKY

The author when serving with the RAF in World War II.

I CHOSE THE SKY

Squadron Leader
Leonard H. Rochford
DSC AND BAR, DFC

With a Foreword by
Air Vice-Marshal
Raymond Collishaw,
CB, DSO, OBE, DSC, DFC

GRUB STREET • LONDON

NOTE FROM PUBLISHER

The style of the original publication has been retained.

Published by
Grub Street
4 Rainham Close
London SW11 6SS

First published 1977 by William Kimber & Co. Limited
© Leonard H. Rochford 1977
This edition first published 2015
© Grub Street 2015

A CIP data record for this title is available from the British Library.

ISBN-13: 9781909808324

Printed and bound in the Czech Republic by Finidr

Contents

A map of the operational area appears on pages 62–63

FOREWORD

This book has been written by one of the most distinguished pilots and Flight Commanders of the Royal Naval Air Service and the Royal Air Force in the First War.

He served for almost two years as a fighter pilot in France with No 3 (Naval) Squadron, attached to the Royal Flying Corps, and later with No 203 Squadron, RAF. This long service on the Western Front was performed at a time when the normal tour of duty was limited to nine months.

Tich was a truly remarkable person. He stood only a bit over five feet and I think I could have worn him for a watch charm. He had a quiet, gentle and unassuming manner but when he got into the cockpit of a fighter he was absolute hell on wings. No one would suspect that inside such a tiny frame was such a heart of a lion. Not unless they'd seen Tich in action as I did many times.

Tich Rochford not only had vast experience as a fighter pilot but he also went all through the dangerous and exhausting straffing operations carried out against German ground forces which so significantly contributed to the final Allied victory in 1918.

I think that readers of this book will find the story of absorbing interest.

AIR VICE-MARSHAL RAYMOND COLLISHAW,
CB, DSO, OBE, DSC, DFC
Vancouver, B.C.

INTRODUCTION

During the Battle of the Somme, in the summer of 1916, the Royal Flying Corps wrested a temporary supremacy in the air from the German Air Force. This situation proved to be short-lived, however, with the introduction of more and better equipped fighter units by the enemy on the Western Front.

Major General Hugh Trenchard, greatly concerned about the resulting heavy losses sustained by the RFC, requested reinforcements of more squadrons with aeroplanes of improved performance with which to meet the German challenge.

An approach for assistance was also made to the Admiralty who agreed to form additional Royal Naval Air Service fighter squadrons for attachment to the RFC.

Thus, in the late autumn of 1916, No 8 (Naval) Squadron was formed at Dunkirk. Commanded by Squadron Commander G.R. Bromet DSO it moved to Vert Galant, on the Somme, in October and there commenced operations under the control of the 22nd Wing, RFC.

The formation of No 3 (Naval) Squadron was by then in progress with Squadron Commander R. H. Mulock DSO as CO. On 1st February 1917 it left Dunkirk for Vert Galant where it relieved No 8 and took over the latter's Sopwith Pup aeroplanes.

This book is mainly the story of No 3 (Naval) Squadron (or, No 203 Squadron RAF as it became) from January 1917 to December 1918 during which period I served in it continuously as a pilot, taking part in many of the great battles on the Western Front.

As I did not keep a diary at the time the story is written primarily from memory but with the help of my Log Book and notes made from contemporary documents of that time.

Although the narrative is almost entirely devoted to my own and other pilots' activities in the squadron I feel compelled to take this opportunity to express appreciation of the quite magnificent work done by our ground staff of all ranks. In No 3 Naval/ 203 RAF it was the inviolable practice to leave maintenance responsibility entirely to the Technical Officers, Warrant and Chief Petty Officers and their skilled mechanics. Pilots were only expected to report troubles. Thereafter the matter was left to the 'professionals'.

Without them we pilots could have achieved nothing. At all times their morale was high and despite often having to work day and night – frequently under the most trying conditions – to keep the machines serviceable the standard of maintenance of aeroplanes, engines, guns and transport was always exceptionally high.

It is with the greatest pleasure that I now pay this tribute to their invaluable efforts.

L. H. ROCHFORD

ACKNOWLEDGEMENTS

My grateful thanks are here expressed to all who assisted me during the writing of this book. In this connection I would especially mention the following: Frank Cheesman, for all his encouragement, help and the use of many documents and photographs; the late Air Vice-Marshal Raymond Collishaw, CB, DSO, OBE, DSC, DFC, for his constant support and the generous Foreword; the late Lt. Col. Y. E. S. Kirkpatrick, OBE, TD, for making available his letters written home in WWI; Messrs H. F. Beamish, E. Pierce, J. A. Shaw, R. Sykes, R. V. Dodds, A. E. Ferko, the Canadian DND, Public Archives Canada and the J. M. Bruce/G. S. Leslie Collection.

The much appreciated co-operation of these donors and friends – some of whom were fellow pilots in WWI – will, I am sure, enhance the interest of the book for the reader.

CHAPTER I

HENDON – A TYRO TAKES OFF

I was born on 10th November 1896 in the parish of Enfield, Middlesex. My father, John Rochford, was one of the pioneers of the glasshouse industry in the Lea Valley. He owned nurseries at Enfield Highway where vast quantities of some of the finest grapes, tomatoes and cucumbers in the world were grown and taken by horse-drawn vans to Covent Garden Market to be sold by Geo. Munro and Sons.

When my father's first wife died at an early age, she left him with five young children – two sons and three daughters. Later, he married again and my mother presented him with four sons of whom I was the eldest.

I was nearly nine years old when I was sent to a preparatory boarding school at St Leonard's-on-Sea and I think it was there that I first became interested in aviation. At the end of my final term, when waiting on the platform at Warrior Square station for the train to take me and other boys to London and home for the summer holidays, I remember reading on a newspaper placard at the bookstall — 'BLÉRIOT FLIES CHANNEL'.

In September I commenced my first term at Ampleforth College, a school belonging to the Benedictine monks of Ampleforth Abbey on the southern slopes of the Hambleton Hills in the beautiful countryside around the Yorkshire moors. Less than five miles away was the market town of Helmsley, where my grandfather, Michael Rochford, had once lived with his wife and family when he was steward to the Earl of Feversham at Duncombe Park.

During my four years at Ampleforth, my interest in flying increased and in the school holidays I often went to the Hendon aerodrome where every weekend public flying displays took place and for a fee of two guineas one could fly as a passenger. Many of the pioneer aviators of those days gave flying demonstrations at Hendon, but I think the events which thrilled me most were the races which took place round the perimeter of the aerodrome, the competitors banking their machines quite steeply and close to the pylons, usually at a height of less than fifty feet. Sometimes there were night flying displays at Hendon and I remember going to one of these and seeing Frank Goodden loop-the-loop in a Caudron biplane. In order that his machine could be seen against the dark sky its outline was lit up by a large number of electric lamp bulbs.

It was in January 1914, during the Christmas school holidays, that I had my first flight at Hendon in a Grahame-White Box-kite, my pilot being Marcus D. Manton, a flying instructor at the Grahame-White School of Flying. I sat in a bucket seat on the leading edge of the bottom plane and Manton sat in a similar seat in front of and slightly below me. Neither of us had any protection from the wind. We flew just one wide circuit of the aerodrome, and the flight lasted only a few minutes but, as the air beat against my face and around my body, I got a thrill such as I had never experienced before and I felt the flight was well worth the two guinea fee I had paid.

I left Ampleforth College in April 1914 and during the summer months travelled daily to a tutorial college in London where I 'crammed' for the entrance examination to the City and Guilds Engineering College and the London Matriculation examination. In September 1914 I entered the City and Guilds Engineering College at South Kensington travelling there daily from my home and completing the first year course in June 1915.

The war had been in progress for nearly one year, I was now eighteen years old and I felt I ought to volunteer for service in the fighting forces. It seemed to me there were three choices, land, sea or sky, and as I was still keen on flying, I chose the sky. Having decided to apply for training as a pilot in the Royal Naval Air Service, I went along to the Admiralty where I was told that they had received more applications than could be dealt with at present, many of them from young Canadians. I was asked to withhold my application until after my nineteenth birthday.

That was four months ahead so I thought it a good idea to take a course at one of the Hendon flying schools with a view to obtaining the Royal Aero Club Aviator's Certificate or 'ticket' as it was usually called. There were at that time five such schools at Hendon – the Grahame-White, Beatty, Ruffy-Baumann, Hall and London & Provincial. After visiting them all and reading their brochures I eventually decided on the London & Provincial School, although their fee was £100 whereas the other schools charged £75. I think I preferred it because it was the only one that did not use dual control, its methods being to put the pupil into the machine alone and get him into the air by stages, giving him verbal instructions on the ground at each stage. Experience had shown that this system was just as successful as the dual control one; pupils learned just as quickly and the likelihood of a crash was no greater. Also, I am sure it inspired more confidence in the pupil. After all, the pioneers taught themselves to fly, flying was very much in its infancy and even instructors still had a lot to learn.

The proprietors of London & Provincial were W. T. (Billy) Warren and M. G. (Geoff) Smiles and before I left their office they recommended to me some 'digs' at a guesthouse called Hatherley, owned by Mr and Mrs Michael, which was just outside the aerodrome in a cul-de-sac off Colindale Avenue. Before returning home I called there and arranged to stay for the period of my flying course at Hendon.

I arrived back at Hatherley, on my Triumph motor bike, to take up residence and in time for the evening meal at which I met my fellow guests and Hetty, the Michaels' faithful maid.

There were about a dozen of us, the majority being flying pupils. Some, like myself, were civilians while others were Army officers, candidates for the RFC, who thought it advantageous to obtain their Royal Aero Club 'ticket' before applying for transfer to that Corps. Many of those who passed through Hatherley later distinguished themselves in WWI and after.

Mrs Michael kept a very nice Guest Book in which we were persuaded to write a few words of appreciation when we left. Many of us also gave her a photograph to insert in the book. I kept in touch with the Michaels and their daughter Isabel for many years after the war and long after they had left Hatherley.

Just before her death in 1958, Isabel gave me that Guest Book which is one of my most treasured possessions. In it is a signed photograph of E. C. (Mick) Mannock, destined to become one of our most renowned fighter pilots in the years 1917–18. Others who signed the book in my time or subsequently were, C. M. Crowe, P. B. Prothero, C. S. Duffus, G. H. Lewis, A. de B. Brandon, W. G. Moore, Harold Rosher, W. R. Snow and the Belgians, De Meulemeister and Medaets. Another intriguing resident was Harry O'Hara – surely the only Irish-named, Japanese, sergeant-pilot to fly Nieuport Scouts in the RFC!

The alarm clock awakened me at dawn. I rose from my bed and, after dressing, ate some biscuits and drank some tea from a thermos flask which Mrs Michael had filled for me before I retired to bed. Then I walked to the aerodrome and reported to Irving, my instructor, at the L & P hangars. The school machines were of the Caudron type, single-seaters with a 35 hp 3-cylinder Anzani radial engine and built in the L & P workshops. The air was dead calm – no flying was allowed if there was the slightest breeze – as I climbed into the nacelle of one of the Caudrons to commence the first stage of my training. This was called 'Rolling' and consisted in taxiing the machine in a straight line with the tail-skids resting on the ground – not so easy as one might think.

I fastened my seat belt and Irving, standing outside the nacelle, explained to me the working of the controls. In front of me and between my legs was a control column or 'joystick' as it was usually called. If this column was moved backwards when in flight the machine climbed as the elevators attached to the tail plane were pulled upwards and if it was moved forwards the elevators, being pulled downwards, made the machine descend. Pushing the column to the left warped the right wing and the machine banked to the left, whereas moving it to the right warped the left wing and the machine banked to the right. My feet rested on a rudder bar connected to the vertical rudders above the tail plane and these steered the machine to left or right according to how the bar was moved.

Irving next explained that when carrying out 'rolling' I must hold the joystick hard back against my chest all the time and keep the machine moving forwards slowly by 'blipping' a switch on and off, so controlling the running of the Anzani engine which was fixed in the nose of the nacelle. Any deviation by the machine from a straight path must be corrected by moving the rudder bar to left or right. He then took charge of the ignition switch, checked that it was in the 'off' position and shouted 'switch off' to a mechanic who was waiting to start up the engine.

'Switch off' repeated the mechanic and then swung the propeller round two or three times.

'Contact', called the mechanic.

'Contact', repeated Irving as he switched on. The propeller was swung and the engine started up. After 'blipping' on and off a few times to check that it was running correctly, Irving handed over to me.

The machine moved forwards but had only travelled a few yards when it began turning to the left. I kicked the rudder bar hard over to the right but the machine continued turning until it completed a circle. I had been too slow in moving the rudder bar and had also failed to maintain sufficient forward speed.

After a few more trial runs I mastered these faults and I was now told to taxi the machine to the other side of the aerodrome with the tail off the ground. To do this I had to push the joystick forward, rev up the engine and, as soon as the tail lifted, bring back the stick to a neutral position, keeping the engine revving sufficiently to take the machine across the aerodrome. On reaching there the machine was turned round and in a similar way taxied back to the starting point.

I was soon ready for the second stage in training. It was called 'Straights'. Having got the machine into position I left the switch on and, as we moved forward, pushed the stick against the instrumental panel. This raised the tail off the ground and as the machine gathered speed I gradually pulled the stick towards me until it left the ground and I was airborne for the first time alone. When at a height of about six feet, carrying out my instructions, I pushed the stick forwards to a neutral position so that the machine continued in horizontal flight. I moved the rudder bar and stick to left or right to correct any deviation from straight and level flight. Having landed on the opposite side of the aerodrome, I turned round and flew back to the starting point. It felt rather like learning to ride a bike or a horse, liable to lose ones balance and fall at any moment. But with each flight my confidence increased and soon I was ready for the third stage which was to fly a half circuit of the aerodrome, landing on the far side and returning in a straight flight.

One of the L & P pupils, named Moynihan, crashed when flying this exercise. In making a left hand turn he stalled and side-slipped to the ground from about twenty feet. The machine was rather badly damaged but Moynihan was unhurt and had already got out of the nacelle when we arrived on the scene.

Soon I was ready for the fourth and final stage of training, a complete flying circuit of the aerodrome. I took off and, as Irving had instructed me, climbed to a height of 300 feet. I completed a wide circuit and then approached the aerodrome to land. When immediately above the hangars, I pushed the joystick hard against the instrument panel. The Caudron dived steeply until at about 15 feet above the ground I 'yanked' the stick right back. The machine flattened out and touched down well before it reached the centre of the aerodrome. I have never landed another aeroplane as I landed that Caudron and it has always seemed to me a very rough way of doing so.

I was now considered capable of taking my 'ticket' so was never given the chance of another practice circuit. I think the flying school owners thought their pupils less of a liability if they entered them for their 'tickets' and got them off their hands as soon as possible.

Soon the day for the test arrived. October 7th started with a calm, dull but clear morning as I walked down to the aerodrome at about seven o'clock. The Caudron stood ready for me outside the hangar. Irving gave me a final briefing and wished me luck. Then he walked out to the centre of the aerodrome to join the umpire there. I took off to fly the first prescribed set of five figures of eight. Having completed them, I glided down and, with discreet use of the engine landed within the required distance of 50 yards from a point near the centre of the aerodrome; so finished the first test. The second, which was exactly the same, was carried out without difficulty. I then ascended for the final 'Volplane' test and climbing to the stipulated 300 feet I switched the engine off and descended (volplaned) to make a landing before switching on again.

That same morning I was informed that I had been successful and in due course the official certificate, No. 1840, arrived from the Royal Aero Club.

Of all the pupils at the L & P School with me, one in particular stands out in my mind today. He was an old chap, more than sixty years of age, named Sykes. We called him Grandpa. At times he caused us considerable anxiety and I remember one occasion when, practising 'straights', he overshot on the return run and ran into the railings which divided the hangars enclosure from the airfield. The machine was considerably damaged but he was quite uninjured. Eventually he got his 'ticket' and was carried shoulder high into a hangar where we drank his health.

We then discovered that Grandpa Sykes was in reality Brigadier General Murray-Hall who had retired before the war. In August 1914 he had reported for duty at the War Office but was told he was too old. So he decided to learn to fly to prove that was not true. He got an army appointment in his old rank of Brigadier General.

As soon as I attained my 19th birthday I applied to the Admiralty for a Commission in the RNAS and shortly afterwards was called to attend a Selection Board on which the president was Commander Frederick Bowhill who rose to Air Chief Marshal in the RAF. Among other questions, the Board asked me about my Hendon flying course. I do not know whether the fact of getting my 'ticket' influenced their decision but, after passing my medical test, I was accepted as suitable for training as an officer in the RNAS.

Early in December I was sent to Greenwich for vaccination and inoculation and quite expected that I would commence my training in the very near future. However, I heard nothing further until May 1916 when the Admiralty informed me that I was appointed a Probationary Flight Sub-Lieutenant and should get my uniform and report to the Crystal Palace on May 16th.

CHAPTER II

THE ROYAL NAVAL AIR SERVICE

At 1800 hours on 16th May with other PFSLs I reported at the Crystal Palace. We were taken to our billet, a red brick Victorian house called Ash Hurst. Here we unpacked and tidied up, then walked to the Officers' Mess in the main building of the Palace where we had dinner.

Next day we started a three weeks' course of drill and physical training, under Royal Marine NCOs with their officer, Lieutenant Jones, in charge. Those Marines were certainly very proud of their Service and never tired of telling us that only one regiment was smarter than the Guards and that, of course, was the Royal Marines.

Occasionally we had a pep talk from Lieutenant Jones and one evening there was a very interesting lecture on ballooning by Mr Griffith Brewer, a leading expert in the sport. However, I was very glad to reach the end of this course and be posted to Royal Naval Air Station Chingford, to commence flying training.

The aerodrome was on the south side of the road from Ponders End to Chingford with the hangars backing onto this road. Opposite, on the north side, was the King George V Reservoir. As my home was less than five miles away I was given permission to live out, travelling daily to and fro on my motor-cycle. The Station Commanding Officer was Wing Captain E. L. Gerrard, Royal Marines, one of the first four officers selected by the Admiralty to learn to fly at Eastchurch in 1911.

We PFSLs were called Quirks and during our first two weeks at Chingford we did no flying but attended lectures in such subjects as Theory of Flight, Aero Engines, Navigation and Meteorology. This was known as 'B' Class, the officer in charge being Flight Lieutenant K. C. Buss, later to become an Air Commodore.

Every evening, when flying was finished for the day, 'B' Class had to turn out and stow the Longhorn Maurice Farmans in their hangars. The Longhorn was a large pusher-type biplane with booms to carry the tail unit and long skids curving upwards and forwards from the undercarriage to which was attached an elevator. The pilot and passenger sat in a nacelle between the top and bottom planes, and at the rear of this was the Renault 70 hp V.8 air-cooled engine.

When stowing a Longhorn two 'B' Class quirks stood one on each skid. This took some of the weight off the tail unit and enabled the quirks on the tail to lift it off the ground and rest it on their shoulders more easily. A Petty Officer, in charge of stowing, directed us to left or right so that the Longhorn did not collide with nearby machines or any other obstacle. By the time all the machines were stowed the PFSLs employed on supporting the tails on their shoulders were sweating blood in contrast to those on the skids who had a pleasant ride. There was always a rush to get on the skids.

Among the quirks was one who was to become a famous figure in the theatre world — Ivor Novello — and who had already written the musical score for *Theodore and Co*, a show then running with great success at the Gaiety Theatre in London. He also wrote the popular wartime song 'Keep the Home Fires Burning'. Ivor frequently played the piano in the ward room while we stood around singing the pop songs of those days plus a good many bawdy ones. He composed a song for us called 'Stowing Time', which went as follows:

Stowing time, stowing time
Makes poor 'B' Class wail.
Other kids are on the skids
But I always get the tail.
Wet or fine, rain or shine
We push those buses in
While flying bounders

Stand all around us
Shouting: 'Tail up and right'.

Ivor was then 23 and very popular with all the other quirks but never appeared likely to get his pilot's wings and, in fact, later transferred to the Royal Naval Volunteer Reserve.

I started my flying training with a flight in a Grahame-White Box-kite, piloted by Flight Lieutenant F. Warren Merriam, and this type, unlike the one I had previously flown in at Hendon, had a nacelle in which pupil and instructor sat. The machine had dual control and Merriam, one of the greatest instructors of his day, allowed me to lightly hold the controls as he flew around the aerodrome. I also did a few flights with Merriam's assistant, Flight Sub-Lieutenant Mitchell before being transferred to the Longhorn Maurice Farman Flight.

The instructor in charge of this flight was Flight Lieutenant Ben Travers who became famous after the war as a playwright and wrote the amusing and successful farces which ran for so many years at the Aldwych Theatre in London. Incidentally, astonishing though it may be, Ben Travers, in 1976 and now ninety years of age, is still writing and producing plays; his latest is currently delighting audiences in London and elsewhere. Travers had as his assistant instructor Flight Sub-Lieutenant Morgan and I was handed over to him. He was a quiet, reserved man of few words and I never saw him smile but he was an excellent instructor being very patient and painstaking. One of the usual difficulties for a beginner is to fly a straight and level course; he is often hamfisted and exaggerates movements of the controls. Morgan had a name for this and would say to me, 'Don't pump-handle'. I learned to overcome this fault by aiming the machine at a point on the horizon and correcting, almost unconsciously, the least deviation from that point in a horizontal or vertical direction.

I did my first solo flight after less than 2 ½ hours' dual instruction. This was just before dusk and, for the first time since leaving Hendon in

October 1915, I took off alone and, climbing to 1,000 feet, made a wide circuit of the aerodrome before making quite a good landing.

Within the following ten days I made several more solo flights each of about one hour's duration and at varying heights up to more than 6,000 feet. I found them most exhilarating and flew over my home and my father's nurseries having a splendid bird's-eye view of the countryside below. My last solo fight in the Longhorn was early on the morning of August 3rd. A slight northerly wind was blowing as I taxied to the southern extremity of the aerodrome and took off towards the hangars. After clearing these I levelled out at about 200 feet above the King George V Reservoir and then carried out circuits and landings for about 45 minutes.

I was now passed on to Flight Lieutenant C. H. Hayward who was in charge of the Avro Flight. The Avro 504 was a two-seater tractor biplane usually powered by an 80 or 100 horse power Gnôme rotary engine. Those at Chingford had the 80 hp engine and, of course, were fitted with dual control. It was a delightful aeroplane to fly, the controls being sensitive and well balanced, and it had no vices. Little wonder then that it became the standard 'ab initio' training machine of the RAF and remained so until the 1930s.

Hayward took me up on two flights each of about 15 minutes duration and during which he allowed me to take over control in the air. The following day I was sent up solo with instructions to carry out circuits of the aerodrome for about twenty minutes. I made four more solo flights in the next few days on one of which I had engine failure but managed to land on the aerodrome although I damaged the undercarriage slightly. The engine failure was caused by a broken inlet valve spring. The inlet valve spring on an 80 hp Gnôme engine was placed in the top of the piston and was opened by the pressure of the incoming fuel mixture against a small spring which afterwards closed the valve again. If this spring broke the engine caught fire and this had to be dealt with immediately by turning off the petrol and keeping the engine running until the fire burnt itself out. Although it was disconcerting to see flames emerging from the engine cowling there was no need to panic providing the pilot carried out this correct procedure, although he was of course forced to land without the use of the engine.

One evening the prototype Sopwith Triplane landed at Chingford, piloted by Flight Lieutenant Hardstaff who was putting the machine through its service tests. It was the latest British single-seat fighter machine, very fast in speed and with a climb like a lift and at a very steep angle. During the summer of 1917 it achieved great success in Naval Squadrons 1, 8 and 10 on the Western Front.

Another interesting event which took place at Chingford was the testing of the Calthrop 'Guardian Angel' parachute. This was a parachute of the anchored type, a line being attached to the aeroplane at one end and to the parachute case at the other. As the parachutist fell clear from the aeroplane the line, when fully stretched, pulled open the parachute case allowing the canopy to fall out and open. One evening I watched Ben Travers take up a BE2c with a dummy parachutist attached by a quick-release arrangement to the fuselage. Unfortunately, when released, the dummy did not break away but remained hanging below the machine at the end of the line. Travers landed at considerably faster than normal speed and the undercarriage collapsed but he was uninjured.

From Chingford I was posted to Cranwell to complete my flying training, my brother Raymond driving me there one August day in our family Talbot motor car. The RNAS Cranwell had then been opened only a few months and was the largest shore-based training station. The Commandant was Commodore Godfrey M. Paine RN who had been the first Commandant of the Central Flying School, Upavon when the RNAS was the Naval Wing of the Royal Flying Corps. He was a big, ruddy-faced sailor. There were two aerodromes at Cranwell, one to the north, the other to the south of a road which intersected the station.

The day after my arrival I reported to Flight Lieutenant A. R.

Cox who was in charge of the Avro Flight on the North Aerodrome. Although I had already flown solo for nearly two hours on the Avro at Chingford, Cox took me up for a dual control flight to satisfy himself that I was competent. We landed after twenty-five minutes in the air and two days later I made three solo flights. After a further five flights, on one of which I made a spiral descent from 5,000 feet, I was transferred to the Curtiss Flight commanded by Flight Lieutenant R. B. Munday, on the South Aerodrome.

The Curtiss JN4, an American training machine, was a two-seater tractor biplane fitted with dual control and powered by a 90 hp V8 water-cooled Curtiss engine. In the USA it became the standard training machine of the US Air Service and was known as 'the Jenny.' A number of these machines had been purchased by the Admiralty for training RNAS pilots and, after being shipped to England, were re-assembled at Hendon where they were tested by Sidney Pickles, the pre-war pioneer pilot.

Towards the end of August, Munday took me up one evening for three short flights and on the third one we practised landings in a field adjoining the aerodrome. Two days later, following some further circuits and landings with Munday, I was allowed to fly the Curtiss solo for the first time. After this I made about a dozen more solo flights. On two of these I had to return to the aerodrome on account of engine trouble and during one landing I damaged the undercarriage.

I wrote in my Log Book that the damage was caused 'Chiefly owing to weak bolts on bracing wires which broke'. Later Munday wrote in the Log Book: 'Correct. JN3 undercarriage on JN4 fittings not suitable for heavy landings.' Very sarcastic, I thought!

The third engine failure occurred after an hour's flight when an inlet valve spring broke and a water pipe connection burst. Fortunately I was able to make the aerodrome for landing, though on one of the other occasions I had to land in a nearby field as I had only reached 200 feet after taking off.

My next move was to the BE2c Flight in charge of which was Flight Lieutenant Maynard. This machine was a tractor biplane powered by a 90 hp RAF V8 air-cooled engine, both airframe and engine being products of the Royal Aircraft Factory, Farnborough, Hants. It was an inherently stable aeroplane with planes set at a pronounced dihedral angle. Not only was it heavy on the controls and difficult to manoeuvre quickly but if stalled it usually went into a flat spin from which it was difficult to recover.

Maynard took me up on my first trip in the BE2c and we practised some landings for about twenty minutes. Three days later I had a similar flight with Maynard's assistant, Flight Sub-Lieutenant Donald, followed by a solo one in a BE2c powered by a 90 hp Curtiss engine which, so far as I can remember, was unusual. There must have been very few powered by that engine. After a few more circuits and landings I flew my first cross-country, a compass and map reading course, to Horncastle, Skegness and Freiston, landing at the aerodrome at Freiston and later returning direct to Cranwell. The following day, in the morning, I made another cross-country flight to Bourne, Sutton Bridge, Boston and back to Cranwell.

That evening Donald explained to me the handling of a single-seat Bristol Scout and sent me up for about 25 minutes.

What a beautiful little aeroplane it was, so different from anything I had previously flown. A tractor biplane of small wing span with a single bay on either side and powered by an 80 hp Gnôme engine, I took it up to 3,500 feet and enjoyed flying it immensely. The controls were beautifully sensitive and balanced so that it felt as light as a feather. After making a few circuits I brought off a good landing and felt very pleased with myself when the Petty Officer of the Flight complimented me on it.

The following morning I took the Bristol up to 10,000 feet and then commenced a spiral descent. It was a fine day but rather misty and when I came out of the spiral at 4,000 feet I was lost. I flew around awhile to recognise a landmark and then found myself over a town, which happened to be Lincoln though I did not know it. Soon I saw below me an aerodrome under construction and there I landed.

It was Waddington which in World War Two was an important bomber station. There was only a small army contingent there in the charge of a lieutenant. None of them was able to swing my propeller but the lieutenant put at my disposal a Ford 'Tin Lizzie' car with driver, who took me to Lincoln to borrow an RFC mechanic to start up my machine. The Ford stalled on the steep hill into Lincoln as its fuel tank was nearly empty and the petrol would not flow into the carburettor. However, the driver backed the car down the hill, turned it round and ascended the hill in reverse gear. Having collected a mechanic we returned with him to Waddington where he got the Gnôme engine started and I arrived back at Cranwell about 1 o'clock. After two more flights in the Bristol I was told I had completed my flying training and had been awarded my 'Wings'.

One of the PFSLs on the flying course at Cranwell with me was Lord Ossulston. His father, the Earl of Tankerville, owned the Chillingham Castle estate in Northumberland where, in its parkland, he kept his famous herd of wild White Cattle which had been completely self-contained for several hundred years. The Earl would sometimes visit his young son at Cranwell and would sit with us in the classrooms when we attended lectures and was at Cranwell to see him make his first solo flight on a Longhorn Maurice Farman.

One evening, I recall, things got a bit lively in the wardroom and Ossulston was turned upside down and ducked head first in a fire bucket filled with water.

From Cranwell I attended a short course at the bombing and gunnery school at Freiston where Flight Lieutenant Morrison was the Commanding Officer. This was a small RNAS Station under the control of Cranwell and was situated at the mouth of the Wash, the bombing being carried out in BE2cs on its large area of sandy beach. There were three stages in the bombing course: first, flying over the mirror; secondly, dropping dummy bombs; thirdly, dropping live bombs. The gunnery course was entirely on ground ranges. As far as I can remember I did fairly well on both courses. Shortly after the Freiston courses I was posted to the War Flight at Eastchurch.

CHAPTER III

WITH THE WAR FLIGHT

I arrived at Eastchurch as a fully-fledged Flight Sub-Lieutenant one afternoon in mid-October. Later that evening, in the wardroom mess, I got into conversation with a 2nd Lieutenant of the Royal Flying Corps. He told me he had come to Eastchurch to collect a Short biplane which the RFC had taken over from the RNAS. Enlarging on this statement, he related the following interesting details. The RFC were about to be equipped with the DH 4 two-seater, a very fine bomber/reconnaissance aeroplane designed by Geoffrey De Havilland, but they had difficulty in obtaining the Rolls-Royce water-cooled engine with which it was to be powered. Short Brothers had obtained a large contract from the Admiralty for the big Short landplane which was powered by this type of engine. The War Office got over the difficulty by buying the Shorts, flying them to an RFC aerodrome where the engines were taken out and fitted to DH 4s while the airframes were scrapped. There was a hangar full of these Shorts at Eastchurch.

The village of Eastchurch, on the Isle of Sheppey, had been the cradle of the RNAS and it was there that the four officers (two Naval, two Marines) had been taught to fly in 1911 when the aerodrome was owned by F.K. McClean. Later, the Navy established an independent flying school there under Commander C.R. Samson.

The Station Commander was Wing Commander A. M. Longmore RN, who eventually became an Air Chief Marshal. He was one of the first two naval pilots mentioned above. In addition to the War Flight there was also the Flying School in the charge of Squadron Commander C. E. Maude and a Research and Experimental Flight under Squadron Commander Harry Busteed who, before the war, had been a pilot with the Bristol Aviation Company. Also at Eastchurch was the aeroplane factory of Short Brothers which was managed by Horace Short, their other factory at Rochester being run by his brother Oswald.

The morning after my arrival I reported to Squadron Commander E.H. Dunning who commanded the War Flight. He explained to me that the main object of the flight was to attack and destroy any enemy aircraft which approached or crossed the South East Coast of England. He then introduced me to the other pilots —Flight Lieutenants Alcock and Henley and Flight Sub-Lieutenants Gibbs, Woolley, Peberdy and Bysshe. Alcock was a distinguished pre-war flyer and, with his navigator Arthur Whitten-Brown, became the first man to fly non-stop across the Atlantic. Woolley, a Yorkshire man, had been on the course with me in 1915 at the London & Provincial School, Hendon when we were both civilians. Since then he had done a spell of active service in No 5 Wing, RNAS at Coudekerque, near Dunkirk.

The War Flight was equipped with two or three BE2cs, an Avro with a 100 hp Gnôme Monosoupape engine, a somewhat freakish pusher type single-seat Scout named the Pemberton-Billing 'Push Proj' and half a dozen Bristol Scouts, all having 100 hp Monosoupape or 80 hp Gnôme engines except one with an 80 hp Le Rhône engine. Dunning said I could have this for my own use. It was not long before I took it into the air but unfortunately I had to land after flying for twelve minutes owing to the breaking of a tappet rod. It was a beautiful little aeroplane to fly and the 80 hp Le Rhône seemed to give more power than the 80 hp Gnôme. Also the inlet and exhaust valves were operated by tappet rods and the engine was controlled by a throttle instead of a blip switch as in the Gnôme. The engine was serviceable again by the afternoon so I took the Bristol up again for about half an hour, climbing to 2,000 feet. The engine behaved perfectly.

That evening in the mess I met Horace Short who was an honorary member. His physical appearance was unusual for he had an enormous head, quite out of proportion to the rest of his body. He also had an unusual capacity for consuming a lot of drink in a very short time. Almost every evening at about 6 o'clock Short would enter the mess, ring the bell and, when the steward arrived, order a double whisky which at Eastchurch was called a 'Hickboo'. In the next half hour he would sit and talk to us and drink at least half a dozen Hickboos. Then he would get up, bid us all goodnight and drive himself home in his car.

During the next two or three days I made several flights in the Le Rhône-engined Bristol Scout. Then, on 21st October, the Director of Air Services carried out an inspection at Eastchurch but did not spend much time at the War Flight. The following day, about noon, a warning came through that a German seaplane was flying over Sheerness. Peberdy took off in a Bristol Scout, climbed to 15,000 feet, but was unable to find the intruder. Later it was reported that when returning to its base it was intercepted and shot down by Flight Sub-Lieutenant Murray Galbraith who was then stationed at Dunkirk.

Soon after this I flew the Avro, powered by the 100 hp Mono-Gnôme, for the first time and after twenty minutes in the air I was returning to land when the engine suddenly cut out. I was unable to reach the aerodrome so pancaked into a ditch on its boundary. The machine was considerably damaged though I was quite uninjured.

In the afternoon of 27th October Flight Lieutenant Hardstaff was killed. He had flown the Sopwith triplane over to Eastchurch to test its maximum speed, timed over a measured mile. When flying at a height of less than 100 feet at an estimated speed of 130 mph the wings folded up and Hardstaff was killed instantly in the crash. I was in the air in a Bristol at the time so did not see the crash take place. Hardstaff was buried in the Eastchurch village cemetery and some of his Chingford friends, including Ben Travers, attended the funeral.

A number of RNVR officers were at Eastchurch on a Wireless Operators Course and at the beginning of November Dunning detailed me to fly one of them in a BE2c to Brighton and back. The officer was Sub-Lieutenant Stevens RNVR, and he was to transmit and receive messages in the Morse Code by the wireless equipment installed into the BE2c. On reaching Sittingbourne on the outward journey my engine started to lose revs and the machine failed to maintain height so I decided to return to Eastchurch, dropping from 1,200 feet to 600 feet before reaching the aerodrome. After the engine had received attention, I took the machine up again on a test flight but the engine, although giving 1,700 rpm, still lacked power so I landed after ten minutes and handed it over to the mechanics for further attention.

Dunning told me that I was to do some night flying and just before 7 o'clock on the evening of 2nd November I had my first night flying trip with Alcock in a BE2c. We took off along the line of acetylene flares and gradually climbed to 5,000 feet. The night was clear with a full moon so I got a splendid bird's-eye view of the Thames Estuary and the North Sea with the moon reflected in the water. I was also able to distinguish towns such as Sittingbourne, Faversham and Sheerness with its dockyard. As the machine was fitted with dual control Alcock allowed me to take over control from time to time during the flight. After flying around for about half an hour Alcock made a gradual, powered approach to the aerodrome, closing the throttle when near the ground and landing along the flarepath.

Soon I made another attempt to fly to Brighton, this time in another BE2c and with another officer – Sub-Lieutenant Haywood RNVR. On the way I got lost and landed in a field to enquire where I was. Finding that we were at Groombridge, I took off again over some high trees. I only just cleared them and, with very little flying speed, this nearly started a flat spin, a dangerous thing to do in a BE2c. On reaching Brighton I landed at the nearby RFC night-flying aerodrome of Telscombe Cliffs where we enjoyed a very good lunch after which I took off for the return journey to Eastchurch which proved to be an uneventful flight.

On 7th November I went home on leave during which I celebrated my twentieth birthday, experienced an air raid and saw the Zeppelin shot down at Potters Bar by A. de Bath Brandon, RFC. He was a New

Zealander and was with me at Hatherley in 1915 when we were learning to fly at Hendon. On my return from leave I went into the naval hospital at Sheerness to receive treatment for scabies which I think I probably caught at Freiston through sleeping in dirty blankets.

Fortunately I left hospital just in time to attend a party in London to which I had been invited by the mother, a widow, of six delightful daughters. It was to celebrate the twenty-first birthday of the two eldest girls who were twins and I need hardly say that we all had a wonderful time. One of those twins later joined the WAACs and went out to France where we met again. Today, she and two of her sisters live in Santa Fe, New Mexico where I visited them in recent years.

On 2nd December I was Duty Pilot, part of whose job was the Dawn Patrol. It was a foggy morning as I took off in a Bristol Scout at about seven o'clock but after flying around for about ten minutes at 1,000 feet the weather became so bad that I decided to cancel the patrol and land.

Our Bristol Scouts carried as armament a single Lewis machine-gun fixed to the centre-section of the top plane and fired over the propeller. On the morning of 4th December I had three short flights in one of these Bristols during which I practised firing the Lewis gun. On one flight I fired off a complete drum of 47 rounds without trouble, but on each of the others I had gun stoppages which I could not clear. When landing at the end of the third flight I damaged the undercarriage. In the afternoon, I was up again in a Bristol and practised Immelmann or stall turns, so called because the machine stalls at the top of the turn and then dives in the opposite direction.

I was now told by Dunning to prepare for my first solo night flight so during the next two days I carried out some flights on a BE2c taking a passenger with me on two of them. In between there was an air raid warning which, like the double whisky, was called a 'Hickboo' at Eastchurch. I took off in a Bristol but was unable to find any enemy aircraft so returned to the aerodrome.

Just before dusk on 6th December I went up in a BE2c and made two powered approach landings and soon afterwards was up flying my first solo night flight. Taxiing from the hangars to the line of acetylene flares I opened the throttle to the full and was soon above Eastchurch village. It was a beautifully clear night and I climbed to 3,000 feet in the moonlight. The 90 hp RAF engine ran perfectly, its exhaust pipes glowing almost white hot as I flew around in the dark, noting the landmarks below me as I had done in my previous night flight with Alcock. After flying for half an hour I prepared to land. Throttling back slightly I gradually descended to a point south of the aerodrome, then made a left-hand turn into wind. I was then in position to make a powered approach to the flarepath. I closed the throttle further but still keeping the engine running at sufficient revolutions for the machine to descend at rather more than normal gliding speed. I reached the flarepath only a few feet above the ground, then closing the throttle fully I brought the control column back towards me and the machine touched down without a bump.

I was now supposed to be qualified to fly at night but Dunning seemed determined I should get some experience of flying blind and, on the following day, he sent me up in a BE2c to practise flying in clouds. I entered cloud at 4,000 feet and set the machine on a straight and level course. From time to time I came out of the clouds to check my position by landmarks and after 45 minutes I landed. That afternoon I practised making more landings in the dusk in a BE2c.

In the afternoon of 8th December, Dunning sent me off in a Bristol to practise looping-the-loop, my first attempt at aerobatics. I climbed to 7,000 feet then put the machine into a short dive to obtain some extra speed before bringing the joystick back to climb vertically, then upside down over the top, shutting off the engine as I went into a dive from which I soon recovered and switched on the engine. It was quite a good loop so before landing I did another one equally good. Not long afterwards I was airborne again and looped twice before landing.

Two days later I made my one and only flight in the Pemberton-

Billing PB25, 'Push-Proj'. This was an experimental single-seat pusher scout or fighter and I believe there were only three of them built, the number of this one being 9003. The wings were swept back and there was a big gap between top and bottom planes, the latter being very near the ground which gave it a very low undercarriage. The main planes had a narrow cord and the nacelle was placed mid-way between them, the single cockpit being well in front of them and the engine, a 100 hp Mono-Gnôme, was attached to the rear of the nacelle. The tail unit was carried on booms and consisted of a tail plane with elevator and two vertical fins to which the rudders were attached. I climbed the 'Push-Proj' to 5,000 feet and found its level speed was 80 mph. It was a very stable machine but rather heavy on the controls and not very easy to land well as it tended to 'buck' after touching down.

One day when I was up in a Bristol, Dunning, flying the 'Push-Proj', came close alongside and remained there in formation for a short time. He was a queer sight wearing a blue woollen close-fitting garment under his flying helmet, in which were slits for his eyes, nose and mouth. He looked like a creature from Mars!

On another occasion he landed the 'Push-Proj', and said to Alcock, 'I would like you to take this machine up and see what you think of it as I thought the wings were going to fall off.' Poor Alcock! I don't know what he thought but he flew the machine and after landing reported that it was quite safe.

Dunning now left us on being posted elsewhere to carry out experiments in deck landings on warships. It was on 2nd August 1917 that he made the first ever deck-landing on HMS *Furious* in a Sopwith Pup but was tragically killed two days later when trying to repeat that achievement.

Our new CO was Flight Commander Bettington who had only been with us a few days when I was transferred to Detling which was a sort of satellite to Eastchurch. I arrived at Detling about a week before Christmas having flown there in Bristol Scout 8969. The aerodrome, on the North Downs and about four miles from Maidstone, was commanded by Lieutenant Commander Lockyer RNVR who was not a pilot. Besides myself there were Flight Sub-Lieutenants Horniman, Ireland, Elliott, Bennetts and Thomas. We were equipped with Bristol Scouts and BE2cs, the former for attacking enemy aeroplanes by day, the latter for shooting down Zeppelins at night.

During the morning of 23rd December, Lockyer drove me into Maidstone in the official station motor car, a Lanchester with tiller steering. We left Detling, on the top of the Downs, in brilliant sunshine but halfway down the hill we ran into dense fog, which we drove through all the way to Maidstone. There we did some shopping and called at the Royal Star Hotel for a drink before returning to Detling, the fog gradually clearing on our way home.

In the afternoon of the following day, my brother Raymond, a 2nd Lieutenant RFC, telephoned me to say that he, my sister Lucy and my brother Clem, an Army cadet, had motored down to Maidstone and were staying at the Royal Star Hotel. The following day they called for me at Detling and we had lunch at their hotel. Afterwards we all returned to Detling and I took each of my brothers up for flights in a BE2c followed by tea in the wardroom before they returned to Maidstone.

On Christmas Day the wardroom looked very gay with the Christmas decorations. In the evening we had a dinner party at which our guests were three young ladies who were friends of Lockyer, Fred Murray, a local farmer who often visited the mess to have a drink with us, and Fred's wife Ida. After a very nice meal with plenty of drink we played some party games. The favourite was a high-kicking competition in which a ball was suspended from the central electric light fitting and which each competitor had to try to kick. Those who failed were eliminated and the ball was raised higher. Eventually Ida Murray was the highest kicker and the winner. She was a very tall girl.

On Boxing Day I took up our only 100 hp Mono-Gnôme-engined Avro for half an hour and two days later I flew to Manston in a Bristol to visit some friends whom I had known at Cranwell and Chingford.

The weather deteriorated so I stayed at Manston that and the following night. Eventually, on 30th December I returned to base in a 50 mph gale. This was my last flight at Detling for on New Year's Day the Deputy Controller Air Services, Wing Commander Smythe-Osbourne, visited us in the afternoon and told Bennetts, Thomas, Elliott and myself that we were to proceed to RNAS Dover on 10th January for a short course before going to Dunkirk on active service. We were given seven days' leave during which we were to get our overseas kit and khaki uniforms.

After a very enjoyable leave I left home for Dover on the evening of 10th January. My sister accompanied me to London to see me off and as we were leaving Liverpool Street Station in a taxi there was a violent explosion followed by a flash which lit up the sky. The explosion was in a munition works at Silvertown and caused much loss of life there. I arrived at RNAS Dover late that night and found I was sharing a cabin with Bennetts.

After breakfast next day I reported to the Station Commander, Wing Commander Osmond CBE, and then to Flight Lieutenant Jullerot who was in charge of flying training. Henri Jullerot was a pioneer flyer of pre-war days and a pilot with the Bristol Aviation Company and chief instructor in charge of the Bristol School of Flying where many of the original RFC officers were trained.

After reporting to his office, Jullerot took us outside to show us the layout of our aerodrome, known as Guston Road, which was on top of the cliffs above Dover. Along the northern boundary was a line of hangars and station buildings and immediately behind them a steep drop onto the town; to the west was Dover Castle, high up on the cliff top and below it the harbour; to the south, below the cliffs, lay the English Channel. Eastward was the RFC aerodrome of Swingate Down and open country, so you hoped that any engine failure after take-off would be in that direction. However, Henri Jullerot did not seem to think there was much to worry about as he said to us, 'So, you see it is a very good aerodrome.'

Later Jullerot gave us a talk on the latest flying tactics. He told us the

RFC had suffered heavy casualties when the enemy, during the Battle of the Somme, had gained superiority in fighter aeroplanes so that it was now necessary to patrol in flight formations usually of five or six machines. We would, he said, get practice in formation flying when we joined our squadrons on the Western Front.

He then told us how we should take evasive action when attacked, saying, 'When you see the Hun you spin'. When asked, 'What do you do if, when you recover from the spin, the Hun is still there?' he replied, 'Then you spin again.' Undoubtedly he knew nothing about air fighting tactics as we were later to find out from our own experience.

During the next ten days I made about ten flights mainly on the Curtiss JN4 and the standard two-seat Nieuport plus one flight in a Bristol Scout. Then, on the 23rd January, Jullerot signed my Log Book beneath his remark 'Ready for Active Service'.

CHAPTER IV

EARLY FLIGHTS AND FIGHTS IN FRANCE

On 24th January 1917 Flight Sub-Lieutenants Elliott, Thomas and I were driven in a Lancia tender from the aerodrome to Dover Harbour where we boarded the destroyer HMS *Mermaid*.

It was early afternoon when we weighed anchor and steamed out into the English Channel. The weather was overcast, dry and bitterly cold with good visibility. Snow lay on the fields above the cliffs of Dover and I stood on deck gazing at them, until they disappeared from sight as the *Mermaid* ploughed through the choppy sea on her way to France.

I was never a good sailor so I remained on deck most of the time though I did occasionally go below to the Ward Room to get warmed up. Thomas was a good sailor but poor Elliott was very seasick and had a rather rough time although he soon recovered on going ashore.

We approached the French coast a few miles east of Calais, then turned eastwards and followed it, about a mile from the shore, until we reached Dunkirk. As we entered the harbour at about 4 o'clock a Sopwith 'Baby' Seaplane circled overhead before landing near the seaplane base.

A tender awaited us on the quayside and this conveyed us to the aerodrome at St Pol where the headquarters of No 1 Wing RNAS were situated. This unit, under Wing Commander Chambers, was in the Dunkirk Command of Wing Captain C.L. Lambe. It was here, during the autumn of 1916, that Squadron Commander G.R. Bromet had formed No 8 (Naval) Squadron for the purpose of reinforcing the RFC fighter squadrons on the Somme Front where it had been operating during the past three months.

Meanwhile No 3 (Naval) Squadron had been forming under Squadron Commander R.H. Mulock, at St Pol, and this was almost completed. It was to this squadron that Thomas and I were posted and after dinner on our first night there Mulock called us to his cabin. Redford Mulock was a Canadian from Winnipeg, the son of a prominent barrister and a graduate engineer of McGill University. He was older than most of us and I was at once impressed by his strong personality. A man of medium height, he had a square, weather-beaten face with eyes that nearly always had a twinkle in them. Later I was to discover that he was a highly competent organizer and had a deep understanding of human nature. His decorations were the DSO and the French Legion of Honour.

Welcoming us, he said that in about a week's time we would be moving to Vert Galant on the Somme Front to relieve No 8 Naval and would be attached to the 22nd Wing RFC under Lieutenant Colonel F. Vesey-Holt DSO. We could, he said, look forward to very hard fighting and difficult times ahead as the Germans were operating a considerable number of fighter squadrons on the front, all of them equipped with the latest types of aircraft.

While the squadron was forming at St Pol, the pilots had been flying Sopwith 1½-strutters, Nieuports and Sopwith Pups but these machines were not being transferred to Vert Galant because we were to take over the Sopwith Pups left there by 8 Naval.

The day after my arrival at St Pol, Flight Lieutenant H.G. Travers, a senior pilot in 'A' Flight, took me down to the aerodrome to fly a 1½-strutter. After he had explained to me the various characteristics of the machine I took it up for a short flight. The following day I flew it again with an air mechanic as passenger. These were the only two trips I made in a Sopwith 1½-strutter. It was a machine which, at that time, was in use fairly extensively by both the RNAS and the RFC for bombing, reconnaissance and fighting. As a fighter or reconnaissance machine it carried an observer or gunlayer in the rear cockpit equipped with a Lewis machine-gun on a revolving Scarff mounting. As a bomber the rear cockpit was covered over. It was used by No 3 Wing, RNAS at

Luxeuil for long distance bombing raids on German industrial areas, the bombers being escorted by the fighters. The RFC used it for flights many miles behind the German lines. I found it a very pleasant aeroplane to fly, something like the Avro 504 though faster.

A day later I flew a Sopwith Pup for the first time. This was a single-seat scout powered by an 80 hp Le Rhône rotary engine and had a fixed Vickers machine-gun synchronised by the Sopwith-Kauper gear to fire forwards through the arc of the propeller. I climbed to 4,000 feet and flew around for about twenty minutes in this delightful little aeroplane which was light to handle and quick to manoeuvre. On this flight I did not attempt anything more than straightforward flying, but a day or so later I was up again in another Pup and, after climbing to 6,000 feet, looped it three times with ease before landing.

Another squadron in No 1 Wing at St Pol was No 2 (Naval) Squadron equipped with Sopwith 1½-strutters and mainly employed on photographic reconnaissance flights. They operated along the Belgian Coast and about fifteen miles inland from it, taking photographs of Bruges Docks and the Zeebrugge Mole to ascertain the movements of German submarines there. Occasionally they flew as far east of the lines as Antwerp. We shared the same Officers' Mess and as the snow lay thick on the ground outside we had many a vigorous snowball fight. Each morning we would all have a rum ration with hot milk to warm us up.

On 1st February 'A' and 'B' Flights of 3 Naval left St Pol with Squadron Commander Mulock in a convoy of vehicles carrying equipment and stores for Vert Galant. I was in 'C' Flight under Flight Lieutenant R.G. Mack and we did not leave St Pol until 3rd February.

It was a bitterly cold morning when, after an early breakfast, we left with our vehicles. I travelled in the front seat of a solid-tyred American Pierce-Arrow lorry which was fitted with a governor control limiting its maximum speed to 20 miles per hour. It had a very good performance in top gear which was well demonstrated on the steep hill into the town of Cassel when it pulled evenly all the way up the hill at its 20 mph top speed. After passing through Cassel the next town on our route was Hazebrouck and here we stopped at a hotel to have a good lunch and thaw ourselves out.

While we were eating, a pilot of 8 (Naval) Squadron came into the dining room and joined us. His name was Traynor and he was on his way to Dunkirk by road. He told us about the adventures of himself and his squadron during the three months they had been at Vert Galant. Although I cannot now remember the details it was quite evident from what he said that 8 Naval had experienced a period of intensive and difficult operations and we were likely to do the same in the future.

After lunch we continued our journey and, after passing through Doullens in the dark, eventually arrived at Vert Galant. We had been twelve hours on the road, were frozen stiff with the intense cold and were now thankful to be at the end of our journey.

Vert Galant was a farm about midway on the road from Doullens to Amiens. Our mess was an Armstrong but constructed of wooden frames over which canvas was stretched after these frames were bolted together. In the centre of the hut was an iron stove with a chimney rising through a hole in the roof. One could sit or stand close to this stove and be scorched in front but remain frozen behind. Our sleeping quarters consisted of Nissen huts each fitted out with an iron stove but the ratings slept in a barn which, they told me, had holes in the walls and was therefore very cold and draughty. They were sometimes also troubled with rats.

The Sopwith Pups which we took over from 8 Naval were mostly in very poor condition having completed many flying hours.

A few days after our arrival at Vert Galant, Wing Captain C.L. Lambe travelled from his Dunkirk HQ to see how we were settling in. He told us that, to bring the squadron up to full strength, a batch of tough Canadian pilots would soon be arriving from Luxeuil where they had been flying with No 3 Wing RNAS.

'They are full out for blood,' said Lambe.

'They will get that all right if they have to fly these machines,' said Casey, an Irishman who was in 'A' Flight.

'The Pup is a very good machine,' said Lambe.

'It is when it's not worn out,' said Casey.

Sure enough, a day or two afterwards seven Canadians and one Yorkshireman arrived at Vert Galant having travelled from Luxeuil via Paris, Calais and Dunkirk. All Flight Sub-Lieutenants, they were H.E.P. Wigglesworth (Yorkshire), J. Malone, J.A. Glen, P. McNeil, J.S.T. Fall, R. Collishaw, F.C. Armstrong and A.T. Whealy. We were mighty pleased to see them and they were glad to be with us after their long journey. After a round of drinks and warm-up by the fire, they told us about the Officers' Rest House in Doullens where they had spent the previous night. Collishaw said there was but little heat and the only furnishings were beds made of chicken wire on a wooden framework. The chicken wire bit into their flesh and they felt like Hindu fakirs learning to sleep on beds of spikes.

The squadron was now complete and the following were its officers:

Commanding Officer
Squadron Commander R.H. Mulock, DSO, L d'H

Headquarters

Engineer Officer	– W/O H. Nelson
Records Officer	– Sub/Lt C.H. Nelson
Armament Officer	– Lt. E.N.G. Morris
Stores Officer	– W/O B.H. England
Airframes	– C/P/O Finch
Transport	– C/P/O Barrett
Master-at-Arms	– C/P/O Purslow

A Flight
Flt/Cdr B.C. Bell
Flt/Lt H.G. Travers
Flt/Sub/Lts F.D. Casey, H.F. Beamish, J. Malone, J.A. Glen, J.S.T. Fall

B Flight
Flt/Cdr T.C. Vernon
Flt/Lts H.R. Wambolt, L.S. Breadner
Flt/Sub/Lts L.A. Powell, H.E.P. Wigglesworth, P. McNeil, J.P. White

C Flight
Flt/Lt R.G. Mack
Flt/Sub/Lts R. Collishaw, F.C. Armstrong, A.T. Whealy, E. Pierce,
   L.H. Rochford

Spare pilots
Flt/Sub/Lts Thomas and Hosken

The majority of the pilots in 3 Naval came from overseas countries of the British Empire. In addition to the seven Canadians from No 3 Wing, our Commanding Officer, Wambolt, Breadner and White were also Canadians, Bell was an Australian, Beamish a New Zealander. Many Canadians had come to England in 1915 and 1916 to join the RNAS and that was the main reason for the postponement of my own and other U.K. entries into the RNAS. We had to wait until they had completed their training in England. They were a wonderful bunch of fellows to be with and the more I got to know them the better I liked them although, coming as I did from a rather sheltered home, they did at times shock me!

I think I was the youngest pilot in the squadron at this time and also the only one who had no previous experience of flying on active service. So I had a lot to learn in the days ahead. Still, I was fortunate to have completed 70 hours' flying time before my arrival in France.

My first flight from Vert Galant was somewhat disastrous. I was flying Sopwith Pup 3691 and when taking off the tips of the propeller blades struck the ground. As soon as I was airborne there was violent vibration throughout the machine and it felt as though it was going to fall to pieces. However I managed to complete a half circuit of the aerodrome and then land. As far as I can remember, the only damage was to the propeller and that was beyond repair.

This accident impressed on me a particular point about taking-off in a Sopwith Pup. When flying other aeroplanes I had always got the tail well up off the ground before easing back the joystick to take-off. In the case of the Pup the propeller had a very small clearance above the ground. Consequently, it was necessary not to get the tail up too high off the ground when taking-off.

As the number of fighter aircraft in the air increased during 1916 teamwork and formation flying developed. A formation might consist of two to five machines. The latter number was usually considered to be the maximum that could be manoeuvred successfully in close formation and was the normal complete flight. If a greater number of machines were required to take part on the same patrol, they were flown in separate flights at different heights, the highest flights protecting those at a lower altitude. With a full flight of five machines it was normal to fly in a V-formation.

Mack called us together one morning and gave us a talk on formation flying, stressing the importance of keeping reasonably close together when up on a patrol. Later he led our flight for some formation flying practice. We climbed to 14,000 feet and flew around for just over an hour before returning to the aerodrome. This was my first experience of flying in formation but I soon settled down and enjoyed it. The following day we practised formation again.

On the morning of 7th February Mack told me to go up for about an hour and fly in the area between Doullens and Amiens to get to know the countryside and its landmarks. I took off in Sopwith Pup

5197 and climbed to 8,000 feet. It was not at all easy to find any distinct landmarks as the ground was covered with a thick blanket of snow except for the battle area.

As soon as I had landed and taxied up to the hangars the CO came over to me and, before I had switched off my engine, sent me off again after an EA which was being 'Archied' high above our aerodrome. I took off without delay and climbed in an easterly direction hoping to intercept the EA at 12,000 feet but though I searched the sky above and in all directions I was unable to find him. I fancy he had crossed to his own lines and was well on his way home.

On 10th February, in Sopwith 5197 I flew my first Line Patrol with 'C' Flight led by Mack. On a Line Patrol one flew backwards and forwards above the front line trenches to protect our Artillery Observation and Contact patrol BE2cs from attack by EA. This Line Patrol lasted just over two hours and no EA were seen. We patrolled over the Somme battlefield, a vast area on both sides of the lines which was completely desolate and pock-marked with shell craters and was the one distinct landmark at that time. The rest of the countryside remained covered with snow until the end of the month.

It was intensely cold in the air at our usual patrol altitude of 15,000 feet or more, the temperature being well below zero. To protect ourselves we wore thigh-length sheepskin boots and a leather coat with a warm lining. To protect our hands we had silk gloves over which we pulled leather gauntlet gloves with a fur lining. Over our heads we pulled a close-fitting woollen knitted garment which we then covered with a leather flying helmet. To prevent frostbite we rubbed whale oil on the small area of face that remained exposed. Even in the hangars it was bitterly cold and quite common for the lubricating oil in the tanks of the Pups to freeze during the night.

On 11th February 'C' Flight carried out another Line Patrol reaching a height of 16,000 feet. The patrol was uneventful – we saw no EA – but somehow I lost the formation on the way home and landed at Baizieux Aerodrome where No 4 Squadron RFC was based. This was a BE2c Squadron whose main duties were Artillery Observation. The Commanding Officer was Major C. J. Mackay MC whom I recognised at once for we had both been at Ampleforth College before the war. While there we were in the OTC which, during the summer of 1912, was inspected by a Lieutenant A.P. Wavell, later to become Field Marshal Lord Wavell.

I rang up 3 Naval to report where I was and, as the weather was very bad, Mulock told me to remain at Baizieux overnight. This gave me the opportunity to spend a very pleasant evening reminiscing with my old friend Charlie Mackay. The following morning was foggy so I did not leave Baizieux until the afternoon. Even then the visibility was very bad but I decided to return to Vert Galant. The journey took 45 minutes flying at a height of 1,000 feet. Following an uneventful Offensive Patrol on the 13th, I was up again with 'C' Flight on 14th February. We were on a Line Patrol and had reached 14,000 feet when three EA were seen well below us. Mack dived to attack and we followed him. He fired a few short bursts at one EA which went down out of control near Warlencourt while the others dived steeply away after Collishaw had attacked them but had to break off through trouble with his gun jamming.

Soon after this I lost the formation and after trying for some time to pick it up again found I was unable to locate my whereabouts. I had been flying for two hours and forty minutes and was running short of fuel so I decided to land in a field at Campigneulles. Unfortunately the undercarriage collapsed on landing. I found an Army Service Corps unit billeted nearby and stayed with them overnight after reporting by telephone to the squadron.

During the following afternoon Thomas came along with a Crossley tender and a Leyland lorry with trailer to take me and my aeroplane back to Vert Galant. That was my last flight on Sopwith Pup 5197 which, I believe, was returned to the depot as a write-off. Maybe this was just as well as it had already seen its best days with 8 Naval.

On 15th February Collishaw, when on a Line Patrol, following an unsuccessful attack on an enemy two-seater, shot down out of control one of two enemy scouts near Bapaume. For the next ten days or more very little flying took place owing to the bad weather conditions. On most days there was morning fog and the bad visibility persisted throughout the day. The Germans took advantage of these conditions to commence a retreat to a new defensive position known as the Hindenburg Line. In doing so they were straightening out a salient for they had probably surmised that there would be a big British offensive on the Arras front in the not too distant future.

Before the end of the month Thomas left the squadron to return to Home Establishment. After making several flights he had found on each one that after exceeding a height of 8,000 feet he began to lose consciousness and had to descend. This was, no doubt, due to lack of oxygen for it must be remembered that in those days we carried no extra oxygen supply although we frequently patrolled at heights of 17,000 feet or more.

Among our pilots the Irishman Francis Casey was an interesting and amusing character. Before becoming a pilot he had been an observer. As such he had flown for a considerable time with Red Mulock in the RNAS Dunkirk Command and there was a very close bond of friendship between them. Like many of his countrymen Casey had to have a particular pet grouse which, in his case, was the delay in his promotion to the rank of Flight Lieutenant. At regular intervals, his anger reaching a high pitch, he would write out a letter of resignation and hand it into the CO's office. Mulock, who understood Casey through and through, would shelve the letter, or more likely tear it up and throw it in the fire. There the matter would rest until Casey's anger was roused again.

He had a fund of amusing stories some of which are unprintable, but there are two which I think are worth repeating. The first concerns the time when Casey, stationed at Dunkirk, was the observer in a Nieuport two-seater flown by a pilot who shall be nameless. They had been ordered to carry out a photographic reconnaissance flight to an objective some miles behind the German lines. When they reached the lines near Nieuport on the Belgian coast the pilot stopped short as if afraid to cross into enemy territory. Several times he flew round in circles but never once crossed the lines. Eventually Casey's patience became exhausted.

Now, in the Nieuport two-seater the pilot's and observer's cockpits were not separated by a solid partition and the observer could stretch his legs under the pilot's seat. Casey waited until the pilot next turned towards the lines and as soon as he reached them he pushed his leg under the pilot's seat and pressed his foot against the base of the control stick. The Nieuport started to dive and the more the pilot attempted to pull back the stick so Casey pushed his foot more firmly against it until the Nieuport steepened its dive to near vertical.

Thinking something was wrong with the controls the pilot became frantic and used all his strength to pull back the stick, but without success. At last, when Casey judged the earth was rushing up towards them rather too quickly, he gradually decreased his pressure on the stick and the pilot was able to level out at about 100 feet altitude on the enemy side of the lines. With perspiration streaming from his brow he turned westwards and headed for Dunkirk at full speed. He never discovered that Casey had been the cause of his panic.

The second story concerns a later period when Casey had become a pilot, the incident taking place at Dover. The other pilot involved, who was the same one as in the previous story, was about to take off in a Bristol Scout when Casey, in an Avro, landed at right-angles to him and cut off the tail of his machine. The Bristol Scout, its engine revving at full speed, spun round like a top and finally crashed. The Station Commander rushed out onto the aerodrome in his car and, noticing that the pilot of the Bristol Scout looked very shaken, remarked to him that his face was very pale. Back came the reply: 'Yes Sir, my face is white with rage but not with fear.'

My last flight from Vert Galant took place in the afternoon of 25th February. I was flying a Sopwith Pup named Binky II by its previous owner in 8 Naval. We were doing an escort to FE2bs on a reconnaissance to Cambrai and along the Hindenburg Line, no doubt to establish what progress the Germans had made with their retreat. We saw no EA but the flight became a somewhat eventful one for me. After seeing the FE2bs safely through their reconnaissance mission, we flew around at 12,000 feet until it was time to return home.

Meanwhile a carpet of thick cloud had completely obscured the ground. There was no gap to be seen anywhere so Mack led us down into it. We entered at about 7,000 feet and soon quite lost sight of each other. Down I went with throttle cut back and air speed about 100 mph, thankful that I was in a stable machine like the Sopwith Pup. When the altimeter registered between 1,500 and 1,000 feet and fearing that there might possibly be fog at ground level I reduced my speed to the limit of safety. On breaking through the cloud at a height of less than 500 feet, I found myself near an aerodrome and was very relieved to see Nieuport Scouts lined up outside the hangars. I circled round, landed and taxied up to the hangars where I discovered that I was at Izel-le-Hameau, also known as Filescamp Farm because it adjoined a farm of that name. I was glad to be down on an aerodrome as I had been flying for two and a half hours and was very cold.

The Nieuport Scouts belonged to No 60 Squadron RFC and one of its flight commanders, Captain Keith Caldwell, was the first person to greet me. After visiting the Squadron Office where he introduced me to the Commanding Officer, Major Graves, we walked to the Officers' Mess and I reported to Mulock over the telephone, telling him what had happened and where I had landed. It was getting on towards dusk and the visibility was far from good, so it was agreed that I stay overnight with No 60 Squadron.

Keith Caldwell, or Grid as he was always called in the RFC, was a New Zealander and that day I had met him for the first and only time.

I was immensely impressed by his personality and during the evening enjoyed a long and interesting conversation with him. Likewise, he seemed interested in me as I was the first pilot of a naval squadron he had met. He wanted to hear about the squadron and the Sopwith Pup and I discovered that he knew our 'Kiwi' Beamish having gone to school with him in New Zealand. Later, Caldwell took over command of No 74 Squadron in which Mick Mannock was one of his flight commanders. During the time he was in France he shot down over 20 EA and was awarded the Military Cross and the DFC and Bar.

On the following day, after breakfast, Major Graves asked if he might take a trip in my Sopwith Pup as he had not flown one and would like to do so. Of course I told him he could do so and he took off and flew around for a short time. Though Binky II was old and not the best of Pups, he told me that he enjoyed the trip and liked the machine very much.

As soon as the Major had landed, I decided to return to Vert Galant. Foolishly, I did not notice that the ground in front of the hangars sloped up towards the aerodrome and was covered in soft mud. When I opened up the engine to taxi out the wheels sank into the mud, the tail lifted, the propeller hit the ground and the machine finished up on its nose as the undercarriage collapsed. A Leyland lorry was sent out from Vert Galant to collect me and the machine and I am afraid I reported to the CO with my tail very much between my legs! It was my second crash within a fortnight and I deserved to be sent home. However, Red Mulock was very nice about it all.

On the 28th and last day of February we moved from Vert Galant to Bertangles. I travelled by road in a Crossley tender with Mack and one or two other pilots. February was a month in which 3 Naval had been settling down to their new job. There had not been much air activity and only two EA had been shot down, both by pilots in 'C' Flight.

Bertangles was a much more comfortable camp to live in than Vert Galant. The aerodrome was good and extensive, the hangars were large corrugated-iron buildings and it had sound, wooden-hutted accommodation for both officers and ratings. Amiens was only about five miles away and was a pleasant and gay French town with a fine cathedral and good hotels, restaurants, shops and places of entertainment.

A specially good restaurant was The Godbert and twelve years after the end of the war, on my way to a tour of the Loire district of France by car with my wife and young son, we visited Amiens and the Godbert where we had a splendid lunch including a delicious mixed grill with mushrooms.

After a frosty night the dawn of 4th March brought with it a cold but beautiful sunny day with clear blue sky. It was ideal flying weather and we could expect to meet up with many EA. That is just what happened.

'A' and 'B' Flights were detailed to escort FE2bs of No 18 Squadron RFC and Collishaw, Armstrong, Whealy and Pierce of 'C' Flight also joined the escort. But I was picked by Mack, our Flight Commander, to fly with him to Lavieville where we were to escort two Morane Parasols of No 3 Squadron RFC on a photographic reconnaissance.

We landed at Lavieville and met the pilots and observers of the Moranes. After a short briefing we all took off and flew eastwards crossing the lines at 13,000 feet. Having completed their reconnaissance the Moranes turned westwards on the homeward journey, with Mack and I following behind and above them and all of us gradually decreasing height.

Over Manancourt we were attacked by five Albatros Scouts and for the first time I was in a scrap with German fighters. They were very close and just above me. I heard the rat-tat-tat of their Spandau guns and felt frightened as I manoeuvred my Pup to prevent one getting his sights on me. Suddenly a mottled brown and black Albatros dived from the right, in front of me, to attack Mack. Quickly I fired a burst at him. He fell away sideways and I lost sight of him as I looked for the other EA. They had broken off the fight and were diving steeply away eastwards.

I joined Mack again and together we escorted the Moranes back to Lavieville where Mack and I also landed and joined the Morane crews in their mess. Mack had seen me attack the Albatros and he confirmed that it went down completely out of control. I felt very pleased at having shot down an EA in my first scrap though I was surprised that five Albatros Scouts had failed to do any damage to two Sopwith Pups and two Moranes. The Morane pilots told us that no attack had been made on them.

On arriving back at Bertangles we were told a story of success and sorrow. On the escort of FE2bs to Cambrai, Collishaw, Vernon, Malone and Wigglesworth each shot down an EA when the Pups and FEs were attacked by Halberstadts. Unhappily, during this encounter White and 'Hank' Wambolt were shot down and later reported killed, and Powell was badly wounded but managed to make a crash landing on our side of the lines. He died in hospital three days later. We heard that the FEs returned home safely after completing a very successful reconnaissance.

During the following twelve days, although the weather was bad, a few offensive patrols and escorts were carried out. In this period the one day on which the enemy was very active was the 11th and EA were shot down by B.C. Bell and H.G. Travers and a number driven down by other pilots in the squadron.

It was whilst we were at Bertangles that we started to have great night parties in the Officers' Mess and these became fairly regular affairs. We invited our RFC friends to them. There was plenty of drink about and the pilots had a chance to let off steam. So, after the meal, the party often became a real 'rough-house' so that by the end of the evening quite a bit of furniture had been broken up.

At one of these parties the pilots of No 32 Squadron RFC were our guests. They were a fighter squadron flying DH2 single-seaters and, commanded by Major Cairnes, were in the 22nd Wing, RFC. One of the pilots in No 32 was Arthur Coningham who was known to all as 'Mary' Coningham because he was from New Zealand, the land of the

Maories. In the Second World War he became Air Marshal Sir Arthur and was in Command of the Tactical Air Forces in the Western Desert, Italy and France during the period from 1942 to 1945.

Reverting to his name, I once heard someone ask him why he was called Mary. He replied it was because his mother had wanted a girl! In 1947 when on a flight from England to South America in an Avro Tudor airliner, he was reported missing and no trace of the aircraft or its occupants was found. So perished one with a magnificent record in the RFC and RAF.

It was No 32 RFC who at one of our parties at Bertangles taught us the game of 'Cardinal Puff'. When we played this game everyone was expected to take part in turn. The first in the queue had his glass filled up and raising it once said: 'Here's to Cardinal Puff'. He then carried out a series of movements with his hands, each movement being done once only. Again he raised his glass, but this time twice saying, 'Here's to Cardinal Puff Puff'. The hand movements were then repeated each time twice. Finally the glass was raised three times saying, 'Here's to Cardinal Puff Puff Puff' and after repeating the former movements three times he drank the contents of the glass. More often than not a mistake would be made in carrying out the correct procedure and in that case the contents of the glass had to be drunk by the offender, the glass was re-filled and he had to start all over again. Very few people got through the ordeal successfully and the game usually broke up and turned into a rough-house after only a few had had a turn.

It was about the middle of the month of March that another bunch of Canadians joined us from No 3 Wing, RNAS among them Flight Sub-Lieutenant A.W. Carter who came from Calgary, Alberta and was always known to us as Nick. Soon after their arrival we had a party and No 32 RFC were our guests. The following morning after the early patrol had got away, Nick happened to be standing by the hangars when the Brigade Commander, Brigadier General Charles Longcroft came along with Mulock and spoke to Nick. Longcroft asked whether the morning patrol had got away safely and was told that it had. He then revealed that No 32 Squadron's early patrol had failed to leave the ground and two of their machines had crashed. Then, with a wry smile, he added: 'I always thought the Navy could take its drink. Now I know it can.'

During the morning of 17th March our three flights carried out an operation to clear the sky of EA on the 5th Army Front so that FEs of No 18 Squadron, RFC could carry out a reconnaissance. This could be called an Offensive Sweep and Escort combined. 'A' Flight patrolled at the lowest height and just above the FEs, 'B' Flight flew above 'A' Flight and 'C' Flight were stacked above them at 17,000 feet. On this patrol many fights with EA took place. Bell shot down an EA in flames, Casey one out of control; Malone was most aggressive and shot an EA down in flames and two out of control.

A few days before the end of March Collishaw got badly frostbitten. Mack had led us on an escort to FE2bs of No 18 Squadron when, at 15,000 feet, we saw two Albatros Scouts attacking the FEs. We dived and drove them down. During the engagement Collishaw's gun jammed and his goggles were smashed so he removed them. In trying to clear the jammed gun he put his face outside the wind screen, thus exposing it to the icy cold blast of the slipstream from the propeller. After landing he walked from the hangars to the mess and as his face thawed out it became badly swollen and his eyes almost closed. He was seen by the MO and sent to hospital and subsequently on sick leave in England. So Collie, as we always called him, left us, not to return until January 1918 when he did so as our CO. Meanwhile, after his sick leave, he was posted to No 10 (Naval) Squadron as a Flight Commander. This unit was equipped with Sopwith Triplanes and commanded by B.C. Bell who left No 3 (Naval) Squadron on 29th April. He was awarded the DSC and had shot down six EA while with 3 Naval. We carried out one or two more uneventful patrols during March and on completing one of these Mack led us in to land at Belle Vue Aerodrome where No 6 Naval Squadron was based. They were commanded by Squadron

Commander Petre and equipped with Nieuport Scouts. We had tea there before returning to Bertangles and, as a result, became known as the 'teaparty' flight. It was not long after this visit that Petre was killed when his Nieuport broke up in mid-air when he was doing aerobatics.

The other patrol, on the 27th, was an escort to No 18 Squadron's FEs on a photographic reconnaissance. Owing to heavy snow storms the FEs washed-out the operation. We then tried to continue with an Offensive Patrol until Mack eventually got us lost and we landed at a French aerodrome, Esquennoy, where a French bomber escadrille was based, equipped with Caudron twin-engined bombers. We had lunch with the French officers in their mess before returning to Bertangles.

Early the following morning No 3 Naval Squadron moved from Bertangles to Marieux.

CHAPTER V

SURVIVAL ON THE SOMME

Our aerodrome at Marieux was on the summit of a hill above the village, the hangars being placed in a crescent along the boundary of a wood in which were the quarters of the officers and ratings.

The German retreat still continued and on our patrols we could see the smoke ascending from many burning villages below us. Soon all was ready for the British offensive and the Battle of Arras which was to begin at Monchy.

This was the month of Bloody April and air fighting became intense with heavy casualties on both sides. On our own sector of the 5th Army Front was Manfred von Richthofen's Jagdstaffel 11 along with two or three others including von Tutschek's Jagdstaffel 12. All were manned by crack German pilots and equipped mainly with the Albatros Scout. We called them the Richthofen Circus but that name was not strictly correct because the Jastas (as they are sometimes known) had not yet been formed into a permanent group or Jagdgeschwaden. That was to take place in June 1917, when Jastas 4, 6, 10 and 11 were placed under the command of von Richthofen.

April was to prove a very successful month for 3 Naval for the Squadron scored forty-five victories and our casualties amounted to less than half a dozen. The first three victories occurred on April 6th when Flight Lieutenant L.S. Breadner and Flight Sub-Lieutenant J.S.T. Fall each shot down and destroyed EA near the Bois de Bourlon while escorting BE2cs and Flight Sub-Lieutenant A.W. Carter sent down another out of control. Then, after two EA had been driven down out of control Flight Sub-Lieutenant F.D. Casey and Flight Lieutenant H.G. Travers on April 8th, the squadron had a notable day on April 11th.

On that day 'B' Flight were escorting BE2c bombers to Cambrai when they were attacked by Albatros and Halberstadt Scouts. Breadner engaged one EA and shot it down in flames. Later more EA attempted to attack the BEs and Breadner, who was leading the Flight, drove down an Albatros and then attacked a second one which went into a spin and one wing was seen to break off it.

Meanwhile Joe Fall also shot down one of the attacking EA in flames. During the fighting, Fall became detached from the rest of the formation and was attacked by three Albatros Scouts who forced him down to 200 feet where he manoeuvred to avoid their fire and, in turn, fired at them whenever possible. Eventually Fall got into position and attacked one of the EA from the right and above at such close range that the German pilot's head filled the small ring of the Aldis sight on his Pup. He saw his tracers hit the German pilot's head before the machine heeled over and spun into the ground.

The other two Albatros then cleared off and Fall decided to fly home at 200 feet. A company of German cavalry moving eastwards halted and fired at his machine as also did several machine-guns. He continued to fly west for five minutes and was then attacked by a Halberstadt Scout. Fall rocked his machine from side to side and then side-looped over the Halberstadt and fired a short burst from behind. The Halberstadt broke away but was soon attacking again.

Just before reaching the lines Fall looped straight over the Halberstadt and fired a long burst into the EA until it dived straight to earth and crashed. As Fall flew over the German lines he was fired at by rifles, machine-guns and small field-guns so, after crossing the British lines, he landed at No 35 Squadron RFC aerodrome with his Pup badly shot about.

On the following day, 12th April, Robin Mack led the Flight on an escort for No 18 Squadron during which they were attacked by enemy scouts. Armstrong and one of the FEs attacked and drove down an EA completely out of control, after which Armstrong and Pierce shot down another out of control, as also did Whealy. During the fighting an EA was seen to fall with its wings completely broken off. This was believed to have been shot down by Mack who failed to return from the patrol and was reported missing. Later a German report stated that he was a POW. Although Mack landed his Pup undamaged he had been wounded in the leg and his foot was amputated in a German hospital.

Mack's Pup was named Black Tulip and of the other machines in 'C' Flight mine was Black Bess, Collishaw's Black Maria and Whealy's Black Prince. All 'C' Flight's engine cowlings were painted black, 'B' Flight's red and 'A' Flight's blue. It is reported that Collishaw, when he became Flight Commander of 'B' Flight in 10 (Naval) Squadron, had the cowlings of his Sopwith Triplanes painted black and named his machine 'Black Maria', as a result the Flight became known as 'Black Flight'. I saw a replica of Collishaw's triplane, Black Maria, at Rockcliffe Airport, Ottawa when I visited Canada in 1972 to attend a Reunion of World War One Flyers.

Flying activity now became less intense on our front for several days. I received a new Pup, N6207, on the 19th and took it up on test and, apart from needing one or two adjustments to the rigging, it was a little beauty with an exceptionally smooth-running engine. My mechanic McGillivray, who also happened to be something of an artist, not only painted the name 'Black Bess' in white letters on its side, but also illustrated the head of Dick Turpin's famous horse.

A few days earlier a Canadian, John B. Daniell, had joined 3 Naval and on 20th April I took him up on a cross-country flight via Albert, Bapaume and Arras to show him the lines.

During the evening of the following day there was plenty of air activity and Casey and Broad attacked four Albatros Scouts. Casey drove down two of them out of control and Broad another which was seen to crash. Jack Malone and Tiny Travers also shot down one EA each out of control on this same evening.

Jack Malone, from Saskatchewan, joined 3 Naval from No 3 Wing,

RNAS and became an outstanding fighter pilot who really got going during Bloody April. He was brave, quite fearless and a fine shot but an individualist and this was eventually to lead to his undoing.

Unlike Malone I was a slow starter, far from fearless and anything but a good shot. So far I had claimed one victory and it was a long time before I discovered that my best way to shoot down an EA was to surprise him and get as close as possible before opening fire.

St George's Day, 23rd April, turned out to be 3 Naval's greatest day of the month and the squadron claimed no fewer than fifteen victories of which Lloyd Breadner's shooting down behind our lines of a twin-engined Gotha bomber was the most spectacular.

At 10 o'clock in the morning we saw this large bomber flying in a westerly direction at about 14,000 feet above our aerodrome. Several of our pilots took off in pursuit but it was Breadner who eventually caught up with it. Here is the Combat Report in his own words:

I saw a hostile aircraft over Marieux and proceeded at once in pursuit. On reaching HA's height of 12,000 feet I closed in on his tail and opened fire at fifty yards range. I fired about 100 rounds and then my gun jammed. However, I had hit its engines and was able to force the pilot to land in a field SE of Vron and the machine went up on its nose. I landed in a field close by and walked to the machine and found three men already under arrest — the pilot and two observers. The bombs had exploded apart from one. I had a military guard placed on the machine and then returned to Marieux in my Sopwith Pup.

The Official RFC Communiqué states that the German officers burnt the machine before they were captured, but Breadner told us that he dived on them as they attempted to do so and, although his gun jammed, they were scared away and the machine remained intact. In his book *RFC Headquarters* Major Maurice Baring, Trenchard's aide and right-hand man, states that he went to look at the Boche machine and that the crew had set fire to it after being forced to land and as it was full of bombs they exploded 'and the machine was partially burnt, but only partially'.

Breadner arrived back at Marieux wearing the German pilot's flying helmet and bringing with him various souvenirs including the black crosses on the fabric which he had removed from the Gotha and which we fixed up on the wall of our mess. The bomber, Breadner told us, was on a test flight and the bombs had been wired to their racks. He never mentioned the footwarmer, the pack of cards, or the cocktail shaker etc which Baring reported were in the machine!

Other pilots who scored victories on this day were Pierce, Beamish, Anderson, Travers, Kerby and Armstrong. However it was Jack Malone on his own who had the most fun. He engaged an EA, shot the pilot and the machine crashed. He then drove down out of control a second EA and attacked a third. Running out of ammunition, he landed at an RFC aerodrome to replenish, took off again and recrossed the lines where he drove down out of control two more EA before returning to Marieux.

One morning about this time Captain Albert Ball of No 56 Squadron, RFC landed at Marieux in his Nieuport Scout which had been badly damaged in a fight with a superior number of EA. Our mechanics and riggers patched up the Nieuport and made it safe enough for him to return to his own aerodrome. Ball, a Flight Commander in No 56 Squadron, always led his flight on patrols in one of the squadron's SE5s but he was allowed to keep a Nieuport Scout for his own use on lone flights over the lines. He was invited into our mess but declined the invitation as he wished to return to his squadron as soon as possible. So he waited by his machine until our men had finished working on it and then took off to return to No 56 Squadron. Less than a month later this famous air-fighter was shot down and killed and was awarded a posthumous VC. He had shot down 44 EA according to some sources.

On 24th April victories were scored by Carter, Whealy, Fall,

Armstrong, Casey and Breadner and there were many indecisive combats. Jack Malone had another exciting adventure when he shot down a DFW two-seater which landed intact behind our lines. Here is his Combat Report:

I was flying with 'A' Flight formation led by Flight Lieutenant Travers above the Cambrai-Bapaume road in the direction of Cambrai. I was unable, owing to a faulty engine, to keep up with the formation and was 2,000 feet below it. Flight Lieutenant Travers and Flight Sub-Lieutenant Casey attacked a DFW two-seater which was flying at about my level. I remained in the sun and dived down with them. Casey turned away after firing at close range. I then closed in but did not attack, still remaining in the sun. At about 4,000 feet Flight Lieutenant Travers turned away after firing at the EA. Both he and Casey had gun jams. I was then in a good position to attack and after a burst of fire the rear gunner (Observer) dropped down into his cockpit but soon came up again and fired at me when I had closed to about 20 yards range. He then disappeared again into his cockpit. I forced EA to land intact. I then opened my throttle but my engine refused to respond. So, I landed beside the EA and we were shelled by German artillery after helping the German pilot to remove the badly wounded observer from his cockpit. He died within about ten minutes. The German pilot was slightly wounded in the head. He said he did not see me approach to attack out of the sun and he thought he was landing behind his own lines.

Soon afterwards this German pilot, who was an NCO, was brought to Marieux and stayed with us in the Officers' Mess for a few days. Tiny Travers was detailed to look after him and to get from him all possible useful information. The German's name was Haas and he was a pleasant, friendly little man with a sense of humour. He was also something of an artist and drew several pencil sketches for us. I remember one of them was of a very full-breasted woman under which he wrote in German the caption 'Double-Seater'. On his departure he said he had enjoyed staying with us very much.

On April 25th Pierce and myself flew to the Advanced Landing Ground at Beugnatre which was much closer to the lines than Marieux and there we 'stood by' to attack any EA reported to us by field telephone from an army observation post. During our first evening's duty, Colonel F. Vesey-Holt looked in and ordered us into the air to check up on any enemy air activity. We flew along the lines at about 3,000 feet and after landing reported we had seen no EA but that large numbers of BE2cs and FE2bs were in the air. At dusk we returned to Marieux.

During the evening of the following day Armstrong led 'C' Flight on an escort to FE2bs bombing in the vicinity of Cambrai. One or two EAs attacked the FEs but were easily driven off by Armstrong and Whealy. On the same evening Travers led 'A' Flight on an OP. EA were encountered and one each was shot down by Casey and Jack Malone. The latter as usual had most of the fun and here is the account of his exciting dogfight:

We were in formation at 17,000 feet when our leader dived on an EA 4,000 feet below us. After he had pulled away with his gun jammed, I continued the attack on the EA. At 7,000 feet three more Albatros Scouts attacked me from above and I could not get away from them. But I continued to attack the first Albatros and he crashed in a field near Cambrai. The other three EA continued attacking me and I pretended to make a landing in a field. As my wheels touched the ground, I saw all three EA about to land. I opened my throttle and climbed into the sun followed by the three EA who could not catch up with me before I crossed the lines at 2,000 feet. Our Archie and machine-guns drove off the EA.

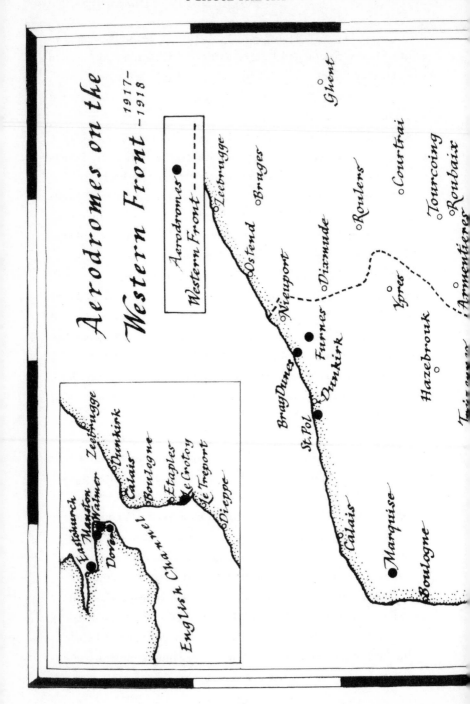

Aerodromes on the Western Front 1917–1918

Aerodromes ●
Western Front – – – –

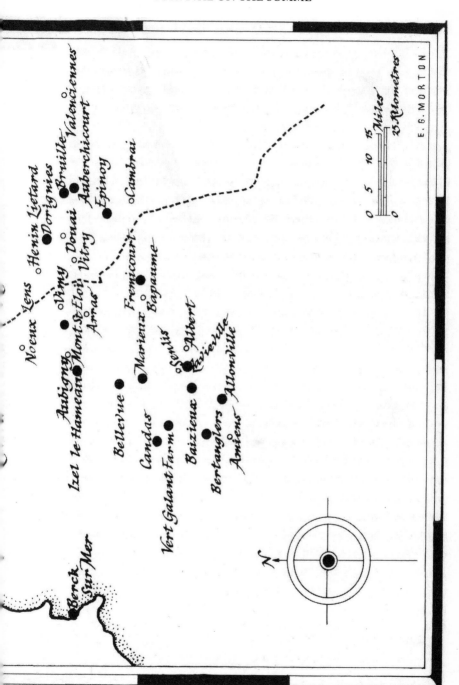

Three days after this more victories were claimed by Broad, Carter, Casey, Fall and Breadner. In the morning of April 30th 'C' Flight set off on an escort to BE2cs of No 4 Squadron, RFC en route to bomb Epinoy aerodrome. Two of the BEs had engine trouble and their leader cancelled the patrol. Another attempt was made in the afternoon but I returned to Marieux after reaching the lines, with a broken centre-section wire. The flight met a few EA and John Daniell had his seat shot away from under him. Somehow he managed to keep flying but got lost and landed at an aerodrome north of Marieux. On his return he told us in his own inimitable way the story of his adventure. The RFC squadron, who put him up for the night, were having a party in the mess at which Dan said he made three speeches, in all of which he told them that in escaping from the EA which attacked him he 'hopped lightly from cloud to cloud'.

Bloody April had indeed, been a splendid month for 3 Naval and several decorations were awarded. Malone got the DSO and Breadner, Casey, Travers and Fall the DSC. Sadly, Malone was shot down and killed on April 30th, the very day on which his award was announced. It was thought that he ran into a large number of EA when hunting away from his flight near Cambrai. Later the Germans reported he had been buried at Epinoy. During his quite short time with 3 Naval he had shot down ten EA and I feel that if he had lived, he would have become one of the great fighter pilots of the war. But he was essentially an individualist and prone to leave the formation to chase EA on his own. This tendency eventually sealed his fate. On the day on which he had pretended to land in a field to escape from EA attacking him, he, Travers and Casey had become split up and all were chased home at tree-top height. On their arrival back at Marieux, a heated argument took place, each blaming the others for leaving the formation.

Before passing on to the month of May, I think the following intriguing story is worth mentioning. During April a scheme was meticulously worked out for an airborne landing on a German

Hendon aerodrome as it appeared in World War I.

This testimonial to the Nieuport Scout was written on the original photograph by Captain Edward 'Mick' Mannock, then of No 40 Squadron, RFC.

NIEUPORT SCOUT.

"A perfect lady" my only love. APRIL TO SEPT

G.H. Lewis, later of No 40 Squadron, RFC, in the London & Provincial School trainer on which the author learned to fly. (*G.H. Lewis*)

Above left: The author photographed by F.W. Birkett shortly after passing the flying tests for his Royal Aero Club certificate in October 1915.
Above right: The author's brother, Raymond, who qualified as a pilot at the Hall School of Flying, Hendon, in June 1916.

Below: Ben Travers, later to become a noted dramatist and novelist, is seen here as an RNAS flying instructor in World War I. (*Ben Travers*)

Top: The Pemberton-Billing PB25 (No 9003). One of the Eastchurch War Flight aeroplanes flown by the author, it was known as the 'Push-Proj'.

Middle: Cranwell aerodrome in World War I. This became the largest of all the RNAS training establishments.

Bottom: The RN Air School, Eastchurch, where the author joined the War Flight following his flying training.

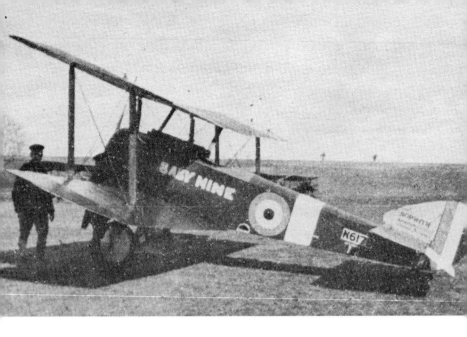

Above: Sopwith Pup of 3 Naval at Marieux, March 1917. This machine (N6179) was flown by several pilots including T.C. Vernon and J.J. Malone.
Below left: R.G. Mack.
Below right: H.G. Travers.
Opposite top left: F.D. Casey.
Opposite top right: G.G. Simpson of No 8 Squadron RNAS on his Sopwith Pup, 'Binky II'. When 8

Naval were relieved by 3 Naval on the Somme in February 1917 the author inherited this machine.
Opposite bottom left: Interior view of a Sopwith Pup cockpit.
Opposite bottom right: Squadron Commander R.H. Mulock, the first CO of No 3 Squadron RNAS in France.

Top left: Mack's Sopwith Pup (N6172) in enemy hands. He was wounded and forced to land by the German pilot, von Osterroht of Jagdstaffel 12.

Middle left: Officers and mechanics of No 3 (Naval) Squadron at Marieux, April 1917, with Beamish's Sopwith Pup. Left to right: Harrower, Nelson, Hayne, Broad and Beamish.

Below: Personnel of 'B' Flight, 3 Naval, Marieux, in April 1917. The pilots, seated front row, are left to right: McNeil, Carter (A.W.), Vernon, Fall, Breadner and Bennett.

Opposite top: A disconsolate A.S. Mather, 3 Naval, beside his Sopwith Pup (N6186) after becoming prisoner of war on May 1st, 1917.

Opposite middle: Another loss to 3 Naval was J.B. Daniell whose crashed Sopwith Pup (N6464) is shown after being shot down by Vzfw. Reissinger of Jagdastaffel 12 May 11th, 1917.

Opposite bottom: L.S. Breadner and his Sopwith Pup, 3 Naval, Marieux, 1917.

Above: A 3 Naval Sopwith Pup (N6195) comes to grief at St Pol, Dunkirk, May 1917. At the time it was usually flown by G.B. Anderson. (*RAF Museum*)

Left: 'B' Flight of No 3 Squadron RNAS, being presented to HM King George V by Squadron Commander L.S. Breadner on Ju 5th, 1917, Bray Dunes. Left to right: Harrower, Hayne, Beamish Glen, Fall, Armstrong and Kerby

Below: The DFW driven down a Adinkercke, September 10th 19 by 'A' Flight led by R.F. Redpath

aerodrome by Lieutenant-Colonel Vesey-Holt with Major Reid of No 18 Squadron, our Squadron Commander and Major Cairnes of No 32 Squadron. The FEs of 18 Squadron were to fly low into the aerodrome at Carnières under the circling Pups of 3 Naval and the DH2s of 32 Squadron. Their gunners would open rapid fire with their Lewis guns on the ground defences while observers, dressed in white overalls for identification, would carry combustibles to the hangars and ignite them with a short fuse. When everything was blazing the Pups and DH2s would strafe the area while the FEs withdrew.

With the element of surprise the operation might have been a success but Brigadier-General Longcroft considered the risk too great as he had to husband his resources and No 18 Squadron had recently suffered heavy losses.

We started May with all three flights of 3 Naval taking off at 9 o'clock in the morning to escort the FE2bs of 18 Squadron on a reconnaissance to Cambrai. 'B' Flight led by Breadner were the close escort. 'A' Flight led by Casey were above them and we of 'C' Flight, led by Armstrong, were higher still at 12,000 feet. There were lots of EA about and 'C' Flight were attacked soon after crossing the lines.

I saw Armstrong sparring with a black Albatros Scout and went to his aid. Together we drove him down to 8,000 feet and there left him to pick up the FEs again. However they were miles ahead of us and we could not catch up and eventually we lost them completely because EA were diverting our attention all the time. Breadner and 'B' Flight were chased all the way back by fourteen EA while Casey and 'A' Flight picked up a wrong formation of FEs. So we did not see 'A' Flight at all.

When we had all arrived back at Marieux there was much argument about this state of confusion which had prevailed. However, all's well that ends well and the FEs arrived home safely and Fall, with 'B' Flight, shot down an EA. But we lost Flight Sub-Lieutenant A.S. Mather who was reported missing in Pup N6186. Later we heard he was a POW apparently having been shot down by Oberleutnant Ritter von Tutschek of Jasta 12 for his third victory.

Next day Armstrong, leading us, took 'C' Flight out at 5.30 in the morning and we passed over the lines at 17,000 feet. West of Cambrai we spotted a two-seater Albatros which was trying to cross to our side but turned back eastwards each time we approached. Eventually we caught up with it and Armstrong and Whealy shot it down. Casey also destroyed an EA on this day when leading 'A' Flight on an OP.

On 2nd May I received a telegram informing me of the death of my mother and Mulock gave me ten days' compassionate leave. On the following day I travelled with George Anderson, who was also going on leave, to Dunkirk in a Crossley tender. We boarded the destroyer HMS *Mentor* and arrived at Dover in the late afternoon after a beautifully smooth crossing under a clear blue sky.

Anderson and I returned to Dunkirk on 15th May and stayed there overnight. The following day we travelled down to Marieux in a Rolls-Royce 'Silver Ghost' open touring car. It took us along very smoothly and swiftly, so different from the Crossley tender in which we had travelled to Dunkirk ten days earlier.

Only two EA had been shot down while I was away on leave, one was driven down out of control by Armstrong and Kerby and the other, an Albatros Scout, fell out of control after being attacked by Kerby.

However, 3 Naval had suffered some casualties. 'Sport' Murton was shot down and made a POW when on a patrol in my beautiful little Pup N6207. He was probably Ritter von Tutschek's fifth victory. John B. Daniell was shot down in Pup N6464 by Riessinger of Jasta 12 for his first victory and was made a POW. On the same day Hubert Broad was wounded in amazing fashion. He was 'keeping an eye' on an EA a few hundred yards away from him and for some reason had his mouth wide open. The EA took a long-range shot at him and a bullet entered his mouth and passed straight out under his chin. He managed to make a landing near Bapaume and was taken to hospital. Another casualty occurred on 14th May when W.R. (Hiram) Walker was shot down in Pup A6158 seemingly by Oberleutnant Lorenz of Jasta 33 for his third victory and was made a POW.

On 19th May I flew with 'B' Flight to the Advanced Landing Ground which was now at Frémicourt. In the afternoon the Wing Commander appeared and sent us up on an OP. We spotted an EA two-seater on our side of the lines but flying high above us. Breadner fired about 200 rounds at it from long range but without effect.

On the following day I again flew with 'B' Flight and at 12,000 feet we reached the cloud base. On crossing the lines we split up into twos and I paired with Wally Orchard. This idea of flying in pairs was Lieutenant Colonel Vesey-Holt's and was supposed to enable the flight to cover a wider area in their search for EA. Its disadvantage became apparent when a pair ran into a much larger force of EA. I saw six Albatros Scouts behind Bullecourt and below me and attacked one of them without effect so I then climbed in a westerly direction to gain height again. The Albatros followed me firing at long range. After a while I returned and, finding them still near Bullecourt, I dived on one, fired a short burst and he immediately heeled over sideways and fell out of control. I found the Archie very accurate on my way home and after landing at Marieux we found that one of my Pup's former-ribs had been broken by a piece of shrapnel.

Later this day Harold Ireland and I flew to the Advanced Landing Ground to spend a week there, standing by to attack enemy 'spotter' aircraft. On the way I saw an enemy reconnaissance machine fly east at a great height over Bapaume but there was no possibility of reaching him so I wasted no time in attempting to do so.

One day, at the Advanced Landing Ground, the RFC Corporal in charge damaged the tailplane of my Pup when getting it out of the hangar. So I rang up the squadron and a new tailplane was sent along with riggers to fit it. The British troops in the area around us were very interested in our machines and during the summer evenings many of them would come along to watch us fly. Usually an EA would come over the lines at dawn but by the time we had got into the air and reached his height he was out of sight and probably home having his breakfast.

One morning Armstrong, at the end of a patrol with his flight, landed at the ALG. There were a number of soldiers standing around and with us they listened with interest to 'Army' as he vividly told the story of the combat he had just had with an EA using the most obscene terms especially when he referred to the EA. Eventually, when he had finished, a soldier turned to me and said, 'I did not know the Huns were still using Fokkers.'

On another occasion Ireland and I did a patrol and were attacked after crossing the lines by four Albatros Scouts. We turned eastwards again, hoping to attack them but they dived steeply away. We had had no luck during the whole of the week we spent at the Advanced Landing Ground.

However we did have one exciting and almost tragic event take place. A kite balloon was sited at the eastern end of the ALG and one afternoon Nick Carter, leading 'B' Flight, paid us a visit. When they took off to return to Marieux I was standing watching them and saw Nick fly into the KB's cable. The cable was cut and wound itself around the shaft between the engine and the propeller. Nick's Pup fluttered slowly down after turning over onto its back and was firmly held by the cable. It eventually landed upside down and Nick unfastened his belt and tumbled out of the cockpit quite unhurt. Even the machine was very little damaged. It was an amazing escape and entirely due to the fact that the 'lighter than air' kite balloon had acted like a parachute, allowing the Pup to descend slowly to earth.

Ireland and I returned to Marieux a day or two later and were replaced at the ALG by Spenser Kerby and Wally Orchard.

While I was away, Lloyd Breadner had led 'B' Flight on an escort to FEs of 18 Squadron. They were attacked by seven Albatros Scouts and

2nd Lieutenants Marshall and Blennerhassett in one of the FEs shot down an Albatros which fell out of control and crashed. Breadner, Fall and Glen each shot down an Albatros out of control and another was driven down badly damaged by Orchard.

During the evening of 26th May I flew on an OP with 'B' Flight and when at 16,000 feet above the Bois de Bourlon my engine cut out completely and I was forced to land at the ALG. Various attempts were made to find the cause of the trouble but without success. Finally the whole fuel system was drained and the petrol tanks refilled with petrol from another source and the engine started up immediately. Subsequently it was discovered that the trouble was due to contaminated fuel and that there were several faulty cans of petrol in the squadron stores at Marieux.

During the evening of the following day Jimmy Glen attacked an EA and followed it down until it crashed and on the same OP Nick Carter drove down an EA out of control.

On 28th May I flew with 'A' Flight led by 'Kiwi' Beamish on an escort of FEs doing a photographic reconnaissance. The FE's leader was wounded and the deputy leader's camera hit by Archie so they returned to their aerodrome and we carried out an OP. I had a couple of indecisive scraps with German two-seaters due, no doubt, to my very bad shooting. The second two-seater was near Arras and I chased him nearly to Douai before I got within range. After giving him a short burst of fire he went down in a steep spiral and I lost sight of him.

Later in the morning we made another attempt to get to Cambrai with the FEs and all went well. There was plenty of Archie but no EA interfered with us or the FEs though we saw several below climbing towards us.

During the afternoon I went in the tender to the ALG and flew my Pup back to Marieux. One of the most important things for a fighter pilot to learn, if he is to survive, is to keep alert and his eyes open to guard against any surprise attack from an EA. Any lapse may be fatal, though with luck he may sometimes get away with it and that is what I did on 30th May. E.T. Hayne and I were out together as a pair on an early morning patrol. We flew along the lines near Bullecourt at 5,000 feet. Suddenly I heard rat-a-tat-tat behind me and quickly swung my machine from side to side while glancing to the rear. An Albatros Scout had caught me napping and was firing at me. Fortunately he failed to hit me, and he then zoomed above me and was tackled by Hayne who 'sparred' with him up to 12,000 feet, without managing to shoot him down. I spotted two other Albatros Scouts below and dived on one of them, firing a short burst but without effect as he dived steeply away. On arriving back at Marieux I discovered my main spar had been hit by Archie.

The last day of the month I flew with 'C' Flight on two OPs and, during the second one in the evening, had two indecisive fights with Albatros Scouts. May was also a very successful month for 3 Naval and fifteen victories had been claimed.

Early in June Wally Orchard was mortally wounded. On the 2nd he returned from a patrol and as he landed at the ALG he collapsed and crashed. He was lifted from the cockpit of his Pup and taken to the nearest Casualty Clearing Station where he died of his wounds later the same day. Wally was a dark, thickset, curly-haired Canadian who had not been with us very long – a friendly, good-natured personality whom I liked immensely.

In the first half of June there was very little air activity on our sector of the front. The German Jastas were moving north to the Ypres front where the next British offensive was to take place. Apart from a couple of indecisive scraps with German two-seaters on 4th June my Log Book shows no record of any other combats with EA.

We left Marieux and the RFC on 15th June to return to the Dunkirk Command of the RNAS, moving to Furnes aerodrome in Belgium on the morning of that day.

During our service on the Somme we had shot down 80 EA and our own losses were only 12. On leaving the RFC we received the following message from Major General Hugh Trenchard, Commanding RFC in the Field:

To Senior Officer, RNAS Dunkirk.

On Naval Squadron No 3 returning to Dunkirk after 4½ months attachment to the RFC 5th Brigade, I wish to bring to your notice the very fine work performed by all ranks.

They joined us at the beginning of February at a time when aerial activity was becoming great and they were forced to work at full pressure right up to June 14th when they left us. Eighty enemy aircraft were accounted for which, with only the loss of 12 machines, alone shows the efficiency of the squadron as a fighting unit. The escorts provided by the squadron to photographic reconnaissances and bombing raids enabled our machines to carry out their tasks unmolested. The supremacy in the air, which they undoubtedly gained, is largely due to the manner in which the machines, engines, guns and transport have been looked after by the flight commanders, flying officers and mechanics.

The work of Squadron Commander Mulock is worthy of the highest praise. His knowledge of machines and engines and the way in which he handled his officers and men is very largely responsible for the great success and durability of the squadron.

(Signed) H Trenchard
Major General
Commanding Royal Flying Corps in the Field

CHAPTER VI

FLYING ON THE FRONTIER

We were now in Captain C.L. Lambe's Dunkirk Command, our Wing being No 4, RNAS, commanded by Wing Commander C.L. Courtney.

Our aerodrome was about a mile north of the small Belgian town of Furnes and on the road to the coastal resort of La Panne which was about five miles distant. We were little more than five miles behind the Belgian front line which was separated from the German front line between Nieuport and Dixmude, by a vast expanse of flooded countryside. A Belgian farmhouse and buildings lay between the aerodrome and the living quarters.

As soon as we had landed at Furnes we received orders to 'stand by' as Gotha bombers were reported to be on the way to raid England. However it proved to be a false alarm. On the following day we were given a rest from flying and while some pilots went to La Panne others visited Dunkirk.

On 17th June I flew with 'B' Flight on the early morning OP over the area Ostend-Bruges-Dixmude-Ypres. North-east of Ypres we encountered a formation of six enemy two-seaters. We attacked them, broke up their formation and one of the EA was shot down by Jimmy Glen. Its observer was apparently killed or wounded and it descended in a spin. The others dived steeply away eastwards.

On 19th June I was back again with 'C' Flight led by Armstrong who took us up on an OP at six o'clock in the morning. We climbed to 18,000 feet and were caught in a thunderstorm after 1½ hours in the air. We immediately returned to our aerodrome where all arrived safely except Armstrong who crashed when trying to land on the nearby beach.

The British 4th Army was now moving northwards to take over the Belgian front from the coast southwards in which area it was intended a British offensive should take place to push the Germans as far back as possible along the coast. The Army HQs were in Dunkirk and the German Intelligence Service evidently knew this because at dawn on 27th June Dunkirk was shelled.

Throughout that day there was considerable consternation and we were alerted in the early morning and ordered to stand by. At 10.30 I took off with Jimmy Glen and Aubrey Ellwood to attack a German observation balloon. We lost each other in the clouds but Glen found a balloon near the German aerodrome at Ghistelles. He attacked it but before he could get to close range it was quickly hauled down.

Later, in the evening, Mulock sent me up on a reconnaissance flight to locate a smokescreen supposed to be covering up German troop movements. I flew along the lines at 4,000 feet south of Nieuport for about half an hour but could see no sign of a smokescreen nor any troop movements. However, throughout the day many smokescreens, both British and German, had been reported elsewhere.

Since our arrival at Furnes a new pilot, Flight Sub-Lieutenant R. Abbott, had joined the squadron. We called him Skimp and he was a tough, wiry Canadian with red hair. If I remember rightly he came from the Yukon where he had worked as a trapper. He had a forceful way of expressing himself, with many gestures, especially when he landed after being in a scrap over the lines. At dawn on 28th June, Skimp and I took off on a special patrol to keep EA away from Dunkirk and covering an area between Dunkirk, Nieuport and about five miles inland from the coast. I saw a two-seater flying eastwards but was unable to identify it properly in the dim light. We followed as far as La Panne but were unable to catch up with it and I thought it was a DH4 from St Pol aerodrome. However, after Skimp and I had returned to Furnes we were told that an EA had dropped a bomb on Dunkirk so it may have been the machine we had seen.

In the evening of the same day I had my first flight in the Bentley-engined Sopwith Camel which had been collected by one of our pilots from the depot at Dunkirk. This was the new type which, in a few days time, was to replace our Sopwith Pups. I flew it around for about half an hour, carried out some flick rolls and side loops and liked it very much. It was a complete contrast to the Pup which was docile and stable with its 80 hp Le Rhône engine and dihedral on both top and bottom planes. The Camel had a 150 hp Bentley rotary engine and dihedral on only the bottom plane. It was an unstable machine and the powerful engine gave it a vicious kick to the right as soon as it was airborne which had to be corrected by using a lot of left rudder.

However, no aeroplane could be manoeuvred so quickly and that was its great advantage in combat. During the several hundred hours I flew the Camel in France, I never met a German fighter which could outclimb me though some of them were faster on the level and in a dive. None could out-manoeuvre the Sopwith Camel.

One afternoon I was taking off on a patrol in my Pup and had just become airborne when my propeller struck the top plane of Hugh Allen's machine as he was taxiing out to take off. The propeller was damaged and the vibration from the engine was so great that I throttled back and attempted to glide across the road running past the aerodrome to land in a field. However my undercarriage struck the top of a dump of ammunition boxes which toppled me nose foremost into a ditch, completely wrecking my machine though with no real damage to myself apart from one or two superficial cuts.

The accident was entirely my own fault as I had taxied only about halfway to the far boundary of the aerodrome before starting to take off. I felt a bit shaken up and to put this right I took Camel B3807 up for a short flight in the evening and tried to loop it but without much success.

Early on 4th July Gothas were reported to be raiding England and at 8.30 a.m. our whole squadron took off to intercept them on their return journey. I had some difficulty in getting my engine started and got away late, never catching up with the rest of the squadron. I flew over Kent, at 18,000 feet but sighted no Gothas and neither did the rest of the squadron. Eventually, after having been two hours or more in the air, I decided to land at Manston aerodrome near Margate. I had lunch in the Officers' Mess and met Jack Scott and Lord Ossulston, who had been old friends of Cranwell days.

I intended to return to Furnes soon after lunch but bad weather set in and Squadron Commander Butler, the CO, would not allow me to leave. So I asked his permission to go to London and this he readily agreed to. My uniform was pretty scruffy and my only footwear was a pair of flying boots but Ossulston very kindly loaned me a pair of shoes. I telephoned my family and arranged to meet them in London where we went to a theatre and saw a play called *The Thirteenth Chair* in which thirteen people at a party were seated round a table and one of them was mysteriously murdered. Afterwards I spent the night at home, returning to Manston the following day.

I had plenty of time to spare so, instead of flying directly back to Furnes, I landed at Walmer, a small RNAS station on the cliffs. Here a flight of single-seat scouts had been established to protect the shipping in the Downs from attacks by German aircraft. This unit was commanded by Flight Commander T.C. Vernon who early in 1917 had been in command of 'B' Flight of No 3 (Naval) Squadron on the Somme front and had left us in April.

While I was having tea and chatting to Vernon, Countess Beauchamp, who lived in Walmer Castle and whose husband, Earl Beauchamp, was Lord Warden of the Cinque Ports, arrived at the aerodrome with two of her daughters and I was introduced to them by Vernon. After tea I was asked to take up my Pup and give them a demonstration of aerobatics which I did by performing some loops, rolls and other stunts. After landing I joined the party again and was thanked by the Countess for giving what she called 'a delightful exhibition'. Soon afterwards I left Walmer and landed fifteen minutes later at Furnes.

In the morning of 7th July German raiders were again reported to be on their way to England and at 10 o'clock we took off in an attempt to intercept them. We climbed north-eastwards out to sea to a height of 18,000 feet. Twenty-five miles off Ostend we saw below us, at 10,000 feet, six enemy seaplanes. We dived on them and Joe Fall attacked one firing into him at close range. Then Armstrong and I followed this seaplane as it dived down steeply, emitting clouds of smoke, to crash in the sea near a German destroyer which opened fire on us. Fall attacked another seaplane, firing about 150 rounds at close range until it heeled over, side-slipped and dived into the sea about a mile NW of Ostend Pier leaving a trail of blue smoke in the sky. A third seaplane was attacked by Glen from underneath firing 150 rounds at close range. This one dived straight into the sea and sank almost immediately, only pieces of the planes remaining on the surface of the water.

During this patrol, on which no German raiders were seen, Flight Sub-Lieutenant Lindsay in Sopwith Pup N6460 had engine trouble and was forced to land in the sea. His Perrin's lifebelt failed to inflate so he sat on the top plane and waved to us until the Pup sank. After that he swam around for about two hours before eventually being spotted and picked up by a French torpedo-boat destroyer. Fortunately he was a very strong swimmer but even so was almost completely exhausted when rescued. The French sailors took him to Dunkirk and saw him safely into hospital.

On the same day at noon we took off again to intercept the German raiders returning from England. None were encountered but three enemy seaplanes, probably waiting to protect the raiders' flank, were engaged in the Ostend area. Joe Fall attacked one of them and after he had fired about 350 rounds it went down in flames. I was flying Sopwith Camel B3807 on this patrol but had to return home early owing to fuel pressure trouble.

During the evening of 10th July Spenser Kerby led Harold Ireland and myself on a patrol in Sopwith Pups. At 18,000 feet off Middelkerke we saw below us a formation of eight Gotha bombers. We dived down on them to attack the rear machines in their formation and as we did so a formation of sixteen Albatros Scouts appeared behind and above us and about to attack. This distracted our attention from the Gothas and since we were greatly outnumbered and the EA had great tactical advantage, Kerby decided discretion was the better part of valour and we made for our lines as quickly as possible.

It was on this same day that the Germans commenced to upset the plans of the British 4th Army. There was heavy shelling during the day and in the morning we watched them exploding in a field across the road which ran past our aerodrome. In the afternoon an ammunition dump, less than a mile from us on the road towards Furnes, was hit. The dump caught fire and the flames and smoke could be seen rising high into the sky. Squadron Commander Mulock, our Medical Officer, Surgeon Lieutenant Panter, and about half a dozen ratings from our transport section, went along to the dump to give all the help they could and did some wonderful work rescuing the wounded and saving ammunition under shellfire.

At a later date an order was issued by the 4th Army Commander, General Sir Henry Rawlinson, expressing his appreciation of their courage and devotion to duty.

One evening about mid-July I got into a Pup and flew over to the little seaside town of Wimereux near Boulogne where a girlfriend of mine, Mollie Cummins, serving in the WAACs, was stationed. Mollie was one of the six sisters whose family I had first met when on leave from Cranwell in the summer of 1916. I flew along the seafront just offshore and carried out some rolls and loops.

Suddenly a crazy idea occurred to me. I would land on the beach. I throttled back, descended and made quite a good landing but unfortunately did not notice that there were some rocks amongst the sand. One of these struck the tip of my propeller, breaking it, and another punctured the tyre of one of the landing wheels. Fortunately the machine remained upright and no further damage was done.

I telephoned the Squadron Office to report the mishap and was told that a party would come along the next day with a new propeller and wheel. I arranged to stay overnight at the Officers' Mess of the Army Pay Corps after which I saw the Officer in Charge of the WAACs and got her permission to see Mollie and take her out for the evening. We enjoyed a very nice meal together at a delightful little Wimereux café.

After breakfast the following day I took a stroll round Wimereux and looked at the shops to pass the time before lunchtime. Shortly after lunch, the party from Furnes arrived and it did not take them long to fit a new propeller and landing wheel to my Pup.

We got the engine started up soon after 3 o'clock; the tide was out as I taxied, turned into wind and took off from the smooth sandy beach. As I did so practically the whole of the WAAC contingent at Wimereux turned out on the seafront and waved to me. Having performed one or two loops and rolls, I set course for Furnes where I landed about forty-five minutes later.

I left my machine by the hangar and walked along to the Squadron Office to report to the CO. Mulock was standing in the doorway of the building and as I approached I thought I noticed a smile on his face. Before I could utter a word, he said, 'Hello Tich, did you have a good time?'

It was typical of Red Mulock. He knew that most of his pilots were mere boys and sometimes mischievous boys and he was always ready to turn a blind eye on these occasions so long as you did your job loyally and well. That trip to Wimereux was my last flight in a Sopwith Pup for, by the middle of July, the Sopwith Camel had completely replaced our Pups. Although the Pup was a delightful little aeroplane to fly, the Camel was undoubtedly a much superior fighting machine. During the evening of 17th July I took my new Camel, B3807, up to 22,000 feet which was the greatest height I had ever reached. I was testing a new oxygen supply apparatus, a cylinder containing the oxygen and a tube leading from it and attached to a mask which could be clamped over the mouth and nose when desired. A valve controlled the supply of oxygen to the mask and this was operated by hand.

It was a beautiful sunny evening and at this great height over the English Channel I had a wonderful view of the earth below which took in the French Coast, well beyond Boulogne, the South Coast of England beyond Bournemouth and the East Coast to East Anglia.

I did not experience any discomfort at this height of 22,000 feet but when I turned on the oxygen and breathed it into my lungs through the face mask, the effect was amazing. It was comparable to an overcast sky changing to brilliant sunshine and I felt very much more alert. It was unfortunate that the apparatus was heavy and clumsy to carry around in a small fighter aeroplane and I do not recall it being put into service in any of our fighter squadrons before the end of the war.

After we were equipped with Sopwith Camels at the beginning of July we had a considerable amount of trouble at first with engine seizures, or partial seizures, due to the breaking of a coil spring in the oil pump of the Bentley engine. Mulock, our CO, was at that time at Dunkirk HQ having been temporarily transferred to organise the reconstruction of the Dunkirk Aircraft Depot which had been badly damaged by German night bombing raids and had been promoted to the temporary rank of Wing Commander.

He met W.O. Bentley at Dunkirk and told him about our oil pump troubles. Later he brought 'W.O.' out to Furnes and showed him the broken springs which had been kept for his inspection. 'W.O.' took them back to England with him and, not very long afterwards, returned to Furnes with a supply of springs made of a different material. Every engine in the squadron had its oil pump taken apart and the new springs fitted to it. We had no more trouble.

Lieutenant W.O. Bentley RNVR had done us a very good turn and we were therefore sorry to hear later that, as the result of doing so, he had been reprimanded for 'short-circuiting' officialdom instead of using the usual channels. Such unofficial methods could sometimes save lives in wartime.

Towards the end of July we started to carry out Fleet Protective

Patrols. Each day the fleet, consisting of two or three monitors, several T.B. destroyers and some motor launches, steamed out of Dunkirk and proceeded to a point off Ostend or Zeebrugge and out of range of the German shore batteries. There it would anchor and the flat-bottomed monitors would bombard German shore targets with their big guns. Our job on the FPPs was to ensure that enemy aircraft did not attack the fleet with bombs or machine-gun fire. We would climb to a height of about 15,000 feet as quickly as possible and then sweep the sky, slowly descending in wide circles between the fleet and the shore, and so scanning a wide area in which enemy aircraft might be flying.

Those FPPs brought me an unexpected but much-appreciated reward shortly after the end of the war. One day, when in London, I ran into one of my RNAS friends. He asked me whether I had received any prize money and when I showed surprise, he told me I should be entitled to some of the Navy's prize fund if I could produce a letter from the Chief of the Dunkirk Command under whom I had served. I wasted no time in going to the Air Ministry where I saw Air Commodore C. L. Lambe to whom I put my case. With little hesitation he gave me a letter to send to the Admiralty stating that, when serving under him in the Dunkirk Command, I had consistently carried out protective patrols over the fleet. Not long afterwards I received eight pounds from the Navy's prize fund.

On 26th July an FPP was carried out by 'B' Flight led by Jimmy Glen. When at 14,000 feet and about fifteen miles off Ostend they were attacked by four Albatros Scouts. Glen drove one EA down near Ostend but Chisam, who was attacked from above by another EA, was forced to land on the beach near Coxyde Bains, his controls and engine having been damaged.

Again, on the following day, 'B' Flight led by Glen on an FPP, encountered a formation of four enemy two-seaters carrying torpedos and one single-seat seaplane approaching the fleet from Ostend at about 9,000 feet. The EA were attacked and driven off towards Ostend and the single-seater was seen to crash in the sea about two miles off the shore.

Just before the end of the month 'C' Flight carried out an FPP during which Skimp Abbott returned to the aerodrome with engine trouble. Later he took off again to rejoin the Flight but failed to find them. When at 10,000 feet over Nieuport he saw three machines between there and Ostend. From a distance he could not distinguish their markings, so continued climbing to reach their height of 13,000 feet. When he was ten miles offshore, the three machines turned towards Ostend and waited until Abbott was within 300 yards of them when they attacked him. Abbott returned the fire, closing to within 20 yards of one EA which dived below him and went into a flat spin. Abbott's cowling then became detached, fouling his propeller and putting his Camel into a nose-dive. However, he regained control of his machine and managed to land on the beach at Coxyde having observed the EA he had attacked side-slip and dive completely out of control.

CHAPTER VII

IN FLANDERS' SKY

Starting early in August, each day one Flight was ordered to stand by all day to prevent enemy artillery-observation machines from operating. As soon as a message was received from one of our Army listening posts that an EA was operating within a particular area, the flight on duty would get into the air as quickly as possible and fly towards the area indicated, climbing to about 5,000 feet. Close behind the lines near Nieuport was an army station where ground signals were put out indicating the direction in which we should fly to find the EA and giving its approximate height. It was usually operating below 5,000 feet, often as far back as Middelkerke, and always flew eastwards when we went in to attack. Consequently we found it very difficult to destroy. However the EA was usually driven down and the spotting operations were continuously interrupted.

One sunny afternoon I spent an hour or so at this ground signal station. It was fascinating to watch our patrols crossing the lines and the German Archie bursting around them. I saw one short scrap between an Albatros and a Camel which ended indecisively and also some Rumpler two-seater reconnaissance machines flying very high westwards towards the British back areas.

During the afternoon of 12th August 'Kiwi' Beamish was leading 'A' Flight on an FPP when nine Gothas were observed over the sea north-west of Zeebrugge and heading for England. Beamish set off in pursuit and continued to climb. About twenty-five miles from the mouth of the Thames, Anderson turned back with engine trouble but Beamish and the rest of the flight continued the pursuit. At fifteen miles from the English coast, at 15,000 feet, they caught up with the enemy bombers and Beamish attacked one of them which was lagging behind the others.

Unfortunately, after firing a short burst, the petrol in his pressure tank gave out and at first, his engine would not pick up when he turned on the gravity tank so he decided to land in the sea near some shipping. However, at a height of 5,000 feet, the engine restarted. Kiwi made towards the English coast and soon saw the aerodrome at Rochford where he decided to land and re-fuel. His gravity tank supply gave out just before he reached it but he was able to glide in and make a safe landing.

Meanwhile, two other pilots on his patrol, Harrower and Hayne, had attacked Gothas. Harrower tackled one and after diving on it several times exhausted his ammunition and landed at Eastchurch where he re-fuelled before returning to Furnes. Hayne caught another about ten miles from Southend but had to abandon the attack owing to jammed guns so he landed at Manston where his propeller, which was shot through and badly splintered, was changed and he was re-fuelled before returning home. It was unfortunate that no definite result was obtained from these attacks because they had to be terminated through shortage of petrol.

In the meantime, another flight consisting of Breadner, Armstrong, Ellwood and Chisam was despatched to intercept the Gothas on their return journey. When at 14,000 feet, they sighted eight of them about twenty miles north of Blankenberghe and these they pursued until at close quarters but owing to persistent gun jams had to break off the attack when near the coast of Holland.

On 11th August Francis Casey was killed. He had been on leave in England and returned to Furnes on the evening of the previous day. Soon after breakfast he took up his Camel and, as was usual with him, commenced doing 'stunts' at a very low altitude. He did side-loops and spins each time pulling out of the dive just above the ground. Eventually he put his machine into a spin at a height too low from which to recover and he crashed in a field across the road which ran past the aerodrome. He was unconscious when put on a stretcher and into the ambulance which took him to the hospital in La Panne where he was operated on at once for a fracture of the base of the skull. He died in the afternoon and that same evening was buried in the cemetery at Coxyde. We all attended the burial service which was conducted by the RC padre from Dunkirk and Wing Commander Mulock, Casey's great friend, also come along from Dunkirk. I noticed he left two wreaths by the graveside. One was from himself and the other from Kathryn Martyn, a young actress who was then in one of the London shows and to whom, I believe, Casey was engaged.

In the early morning of 16th August two Special Missions were carried out by Flight Sub-Lieutenants Abbott and Hayne. Abbott took off from Furnes at 4.15 a.m. for a low-level attack on Snelleghem aerodrome. He flew out to sea, then turned and approached the coast at 6,000 feet above the clouds. Descending through a gap in the clouds he found himself above a canal which he thought was the Ostend-Bruges Canal but which happened to be the Zeebrugge-Ghent Canal. Owing to the very bad visibility he failed to find Snelleghem, but eventually found an aerodrome at Uitkerke. This one he attacked, firing about 500 rounds into the hangars which were of the Bessoneaux type, seven of them being close together. He then flew out to sea but later returned and fired his remaining rounds of ammunition into the enemy trenches east of Nieuport before returning to Furnes.

Hayne left Furnes half an hour later than Abbott, his objective being a low-level attack on Sparappelhoek aerodrome. He flew out to sea and later re-crossed the coast at 6,000 feet, west of Ostend, descending below the clouds to 2,000 feet. Visibility was bad but he picked up the aerodrome and attacked it, firing into the hangars which were of steel construction and painted black. He fired at three Albatros Scouts on the ground and also the living quarters on the north side of the aerodrome. Eventually he flew at a height of 50 to 100 feet along the road to Ostend on which he saw a horse-drawn waggon and gave that a few bursts following this with an attack on the guard at a railway crossing before reaching the Ostend-Nieuport Canal. He then flew to Middelkerke where he shot up horse-drawn vehicles on the seafront. There seemed to be no drivers near and the horses stampeded. He finally landed at Furnes at about 6 a.m.

The following day Skimp Abbott, when on patrol with his formation, was attacked by an EA and wounded. However, he was able to return to the aerodrome where he made a safe landing and was then sent to hospital. On the same day Joe Fall attacked an EA and saw his tracer bullets enter the fuselage near the cockpit. The EA side-slipped and nose-dived completely out of control, disappearing through the clouds.

One afternoon, a few days before the end of August, we were about to have tea when we heard loud explosions from the direction of the aerodrome. The Germans were straffing us and one or two shells exploded very near the hangars. Another landed in the farmyard between our quarters and the aerodrome. In the middle of this yard was a dome-shaped stone dog-kennel, outside which an old mongrel dog was chained. The shell, on exploding, completely demolished this kennel but the dog remained fastened by his chain and was quite unhurt.

All pilots proceeded at once to the aerodrome where the aeroplanes were lined up outside the hangars. Each of us climbed into his machine and as soon as the engine was started up, got into the air without further delay and flew to Dunkirk, landing at the St Pol aerodrome where we stayed the night. Fortunately there were no casualties at Furnes.

The following morning we took off to return to Furnes. Unfortunately one of our new pilots, named Amos, having only just cleared a sand dune at the far side of the aerodrome, stalled and crashed. The machine was written-off, and Amos – although not very badly injured – was taken to hospital.

On an FPP on 3rd September Breadner and his Flight encountered a formation of four Albatros Scouts. He attacked one of the EA and shot it down out of control. Soon afterwards the Flight met another formation of five Albatros and Breadner shot at one which broke up in mid-air. Yet another of the type was sent down out of control by Chisam.

During the mornings of 4th and 5th, 'C' Flight, led by Armstrong, escorted DH4s of 5 Naval Squadron to bomb the docks at Bruges. On each occasion the mission was carried out successfully and without any interference from enemy aircraft, although a fair amount of 'Archie' was put up at us. We, in our Camels, flew at 17,000 feet and the DH4s about 1,000 feet or so below us.

The docks at Bruges were a very important 'military' target since it was from them that marauding German submarines went forth into the North Sea after refuelling and any necessary repairs and maintenance had been completed. Bruges is a very beautiful Belgian mediaeval town and one always hoped that the damage done on these bombing raids was confined to the docks. However, I sometimes have my doubts because about ten years after the war I was having a meal in a Bruges restaurant and mentioned the raids to the waiter. He said nothing but gave me a very black look!

In the afternoon of 5th September an Offensive Sweep of the area Ostend-Thorout-Bruges was carried out by 'A' and 'C' Flights and when near Middelkerke a formation of Albatros Scouts was encountered and attacked. The fight was short and sharp and Beamish shot down one EA out of control and I attacked another which went down in a steep dive emitting clouds of smoke. The other four EA were driven down by other pilots.

Orders had now been received for our squadron to move on the 6th September from Furnes to Bray Dunes, an aerodrome about five miles west of Furnes and just on the French side of the border. The move was duly carried out and I landed there after an uneventful early morning Offensive Sweep with 'C' Flight but after touching down one of my landing wheels was shed, the machine tipping up on its nose. Fortunately the damage was only slight.

We were very busy all that day preparing a suitable road into the camp for our lorries as the ground was in a very boggy state. Also, we had returned to living under canvas, having a marquee for a mess and bell tents for sleeping. There was plenty of mud about but we managed to scrounge some duckboards from an unoccupied camp a short distance up the road and these we laid down for pathways.

I am sure that the pilots concerned must experience a special feeling of elation when they have forced an enemy aircraft to land intact on their own side of the lines. Thus it happened that during the evening of 10th September, Flight Lieutenant Redpath when leading 'A' Flight on an FPP, intercepted a two-seater DFW which was returning at about 15,000 feet from a reconnaissance flight. Redpath and his flight attacked and forced it to land intact in a field between Furnes and Adinkerke. The pilot was unhurt but the observer was wounded and died later in hospital. Breadner, who was still our acting CO in the absence of Mulock, sent out a party with CPO Finch to dismantle the DFW and bring it back to Bray Dunes that same evening. There were several bullet holes in the wings and fuselage and one through the radiator but the damage was not really very serious and within a few days it had all been repaired and, the British roundels having replaced the German crosses on the fuselage and planes, we were able to fly it.

During the morning of 11th September we escorted DH4s of 5 Naval Squadron to bomb Bruges Docks and several combats took place with enemy aircraft. I attacked an Albatros Scout which was attacking a DH4 and shot him down completely out of control while Breadner and Sands also shot down EA as also did Flight Commander Le Mesurier, the leader of the 5 Naval formation. It is also probable that at least two more EA were shot down.

On the following morning the DH4s went out again to bomb Zeebrugge and on this occasion we combined our escort with an Offensive Sweep. When over Westende we saw some Albatros Scouts a mile or so inland. One of them dived towards the coast and I attacked him head-on, firing a short burst before he passed beneath me. I then saw three more EA flying towards me so turned westwards and tried to outclimb them. When I again turned eastwards, they were no longer within sight. On this same patrol Armstrong and Ireland also attacked Albatros Scouts and drove them down.

At noon on 16th September Armstrong led 'C' Flight on an OP and at 15,000 feet we encountered seven Albatros Scouts east of Dixmude. We attacked and drove them out of the sky. Armstrong fired about a hundred rounds into one which heeled over, sideslipped and then went into a spin. He then attacked another EA, firing about 200 rounds at close range and it turned on its back, side-slipped and then dived vertically.

The captured DFW remained with us at Bray Dunes for two weeks. All our pilots flew it and some did so on several occasions. On each flight we usually took with us in the observer's cockpit two members of the ground staff and eventually everyone had a joyride in it. After the Sopwith Camel, the DFW was a very cumbersome aeroplane to handle. The controls were heavy to operate, the lateral control being particularly bad in this respect. However, the big water-cooled Benz engine seemed exceptionally good and ran extremely smoothly. Eventually orders were received to deliver it to RNAS Dover.

We drew lots to decide who should be the pilot and observer on this trip and I got the lucky card for pilot and Harry Chisam that for observer. Our Armament Officer had a machine-gun fitted to the mounting in the observer's cockpit so that Harry could warn off any enthusiastic scout pilot who might not see the British markings and think he had an easy Hun to shoot down in the Channel.

On the day before our trip to Dover, I was flying with 'C' Flight led by Armstrong in search of enemy artillery-observation aeroplanes, when I saw a two-seater DFW flying at 5,000 feet south of Middelkerke and tried to attract Armstrong's attention. Failing to do so, I turned towards the EA which was then flying over the beach and heading westwards. When I was about 300 yards from the EA it turned eastwards again and flew slightly inland. I then observed four Albatros Scouts approaching from the east but, getting within about 150 yards of the DFW, I opened fire and saw tracers enter its fuselage before it went into a very steep dive. I was then attacked by the four Albatros Scouts but succeeded in evading them and they left me when I eventually reached the lines.

Meanwhile Armstrong, Ireland and Bawlf observed at least fifteen Albatros Scouts in three formations coming from the direction of Dixmude. When they were over Middelkerke a general engagement took place and the EA were driven down. During this engagement 'C' Flight had been joined by 'A' and 'B' Flights in response to a signal received from the ground station that 22 EA had been observed flying towards Nieuport from Dixmude. Flight Sub-Lieutenant Harrower attacked an EA with a long burst of fire at close range and it turned over and fell out of control. He was attacked by another EA and wounded in the leg but was able to return to Bray Dunes and make a safe landing. From there he was taken to hospital in Dunkirk. Flight Lieutenant Beamish drove down two EA, one of which went into a spin.

It was 12.45 p.m. on 24th September when I took off from Bray Dunes with Harry Chisam in the DFW. I flew along the coast, gradually climbing, towards Calais where, at 9,000 feet, I turned seawards and made for Dover. Nothing unusual happened until we were near the English coast when a Sopwith Camel approached and circled round us several times. Once or twice he dived on us but it was obvious that he realized we were not an EA and knew of the signal that had been sent out before we left Bray Dunes informing all concerned of the necessary details of this flight, and eventually he left us. We landed at Dover after a flight of about one hour, handed over the DFW and collected a couple of Sopwith Camels to deliver to Dunkirk.

Harry and I took off from Dover in the Camels but did not return immediately to Dunkirk. Instead we flew along the coast and landed at Walmer to visit our friends in the RNAS Flight there. One of them was R.A. Little, an Australian, whom I had first met at Hendon in 1915 when we were both civilians learning to fly there. He had been in 8 Naval Squadron flying Sopwith Pups when they were at Vert Galant and later when they were re-equipped with Sopwith Triplanes. Little had already made a name for himself having shot down 37 EA and been awarded the DSO and Bar and the DSC and Bar. He told us he was the pilot of the Camel which had dived on our DFW as we approached Dover. In March 1918 he joined our squadron in France.

Chisam and I shortly returned to Bray Dunes where the remaining few days of the month proved uneventful.

The British offensive in Flanders, of which the objectives were the capture of all the sea bases on the Belgian coast, had been a failure and by the beginning of October plans had been made for an attack near Cambrai by a massed force of tanks. But desultory fighting continued throughout the month, mainly with the object of distracting the enemy.

In the afternoon of 1st October Hayne and myself accompanied Beamish on a Fleet Protective Patrol. Beamish developed engine trouble and returned to Bray Dunes but Hayne and myself carried on the patrol. When over the sea off Nieuport we saw a two-seater DFW flying at 7,000 feet about three miles off the coast. We attacked and drove him down to 1,500 feet over Westende but unfortunately we both had gun jams and he was able to continue diving away from us inland. The observer was probably killed or wounded as he had suddenly ceased firing at us during the chase.

For the next ten days we had very bad weather and flying was impossible, but during the morning of the 11th we escorted DH4s to bomb Bruges Docks. We flew at 17,000 feet and the cold was intense.

Two days later Armstrong left us for three months' leave in Canada and I took over 'C' Flight. It was the policy of Captain Lambe to send the Canadian pilots from time to time on a long leave to their own country and they thoroughly deserved it.

I led 'C' Flight on an OP in the afternoon of the 14th. At 16,000 feet I saw ten Albatros Scouts near Ostend and chased after them. Three more then appeared above us and we climbed above them before attacking. However, before we could close to firing range they spotted us and all rapidly dived steeply away eastwards.

Now and again during one's flying career an amusing incident happens that might have ended in tragedy. So it was that during one October afternoon we were flying on an OP with 'A' Flight led by 'Kiwi' Beamish when, just after he became airborne, one of his landing wheels dropped off and fell on the aerodrome. Hayne and I, flying on either side of Beamish, did everything possible to attract his attention by waving our arms and pointing at his undercarriage. He however, thought that we were pointing out some EA flying below us and kept diving down to see where they could be.

On our return to Bray Dunes at the end of our otherwise uneventful patrol, Flight Sub-Lieutenant Sands was flying round the aerodrome in a Camel on the side of which were the words 'WHEEL OFF' in large letters and this was seen by us all except Beamish. In addition, people were standing on the aerodrome waving wheels above their heads to attract his attention. But he quite failed to notice any of these warnings and approached the ground making a perfect landing at the slowest possible speed; his Camel then turned over onto its back. He was quite uninjured and the machine suffered very little damage.

Never had I had such an easy chance of shooting down an EA as occurred on the early morning of 18th October, when I was leading 'C' Flight on an OP. We were flying at 16,000 feet when I saw a formation of five Albatros Scouts below. They were to the east of us and flying towards Middelkerke. I led my flight eastwards and eventually got them between us and the lines as they turned and flew westwards. They had not seen us and we could now approach them from out of the sun. Having decided to attack them when they were nearly over the flooded area near Nieuport I dived on one EA holding my fire until I was almost colliding with his tail – I was never closer to an EA. I pressed the trigger to shoot him down but nothing happened. It was a very cold morning and both guns were frozen up although during the patrol I had fired short bursts from time to time to try to prevent this happening. The pilot of the EA, when he turned his head round and saw me on his tail, must have realised my predicament because he turned slowly to the right and as he passed, flying in the opposite direction, he took a good look at me and then flew eastwards in a shallow dive.

The rest of my flight also had this trouble with their guns, so we did not manage to shoot down a single EA of that enemy formation.

At two o'clock in the afternoon, a few days later, a signal was received that two enemy artillery-spotting machines were flying at 4,000 feet between Middelkerke and Slype. I took 'C' Flight out to attack them and we climbed to 6,000 feet from where we saw two DFW artillery-spotters operating at 4,000 feet precisely as had been reported. I allowed them to reach the point on their patrol nearest to the lines. We then attacked them firing first at one and then at the other as they dived down to 2,000 feet at which height the one I was attacking turned sharply to the left and, as he dived underneath me, I lost sight of him. However, I may have got him as I did not see him again and he stopped operating. The other DFW was now east of Ostend but later turned west again. Finally, immediately we approached him he dived steeply away eastwards.

During the remaining days of October routine, uneventful OPs took place except that on the 27th I flew Beamish's Camel to Walmer and left it at the aerodrome there to which our squadron was about to move in a few days' time. I returned to Bray Dunes on the following day, crossing the Channel from Dover to Dunkirk in a destroyer.

At 11 o'clock on 4th November the pilots of No 3 (Naval) Squadron took off from Bray Dunes and one hour later all had landed at Walmer.

CHAPTER VIII

RESPITE AND RETURN

The history of Walmer aerodrome is very interesting. One afternoon Captain C. L. Lambe received a telephone message from the Admiralty that an aerodrome must be found close to the Downs as a protection against attacks by German aeroplanes on shipping in that part of the Channel. The Germans had already made sorties with two torpedo-carrying seaplanes and had, indeed, torpedoed a ship at the northern end of the Downs. A site for the aerodrome was found without undue difficulty, but to find pilots was a much greater problem because all the fighter pilots were in naval squadrons supporting the hard-pressed RFC on the Western Front. However a Flight had to be formed for Walmer so Captain Lambe decided to select six good pilots, who needed a rest after serving in France for many months, and to bring these back to Walmer as the flying personnel.

The majority of these RNAS pilots were originally from overseas. They were largely Canadians, but others came from South Africa, Australia, New Zealand and various colonies. So the rest at Walmer also enabled them to obtain some idea of home life in England and English hospitality. Later it was decided to post to Walmer, in rotation, complete squadrons and so give them two month's rest there. No 3 Naval was the first squadron to be selected.

I understand that in the RFC a pilot was usually transferred to Home Establishment following a spell of six to eight months flying in a Western Front squadron. No such policy was pursued by the RNAS and 3 Naval/203 RAF were engaged on operations, continuously, from February 1917 until November 1918 during which time not a single pilot left for H. E. through physical or mental stress reasons.

We had several long-serving pilots in the squadron; others completed extended tours of duty after being posted to units elsewhere in the BEF or overseas.

In these circumstances the less hazardous duties at Walmer afforded a welcome rest and was, undoubtedly, most beneficial to pilots and ground staff alike.

The aerodrome, situated on the cliff-top at Hawks Hill Farm, virtually overlooked their patrol area. The Officers' Mess and living quarters were in the village in a large and comfortable Victorian house within its own grounds and named St Clair. The ratings were quartered amongst houses in the village which had been taken over by the Admiralty.

Before we moved to Walmer, Lloyd Breadner had been confirmed in the rank of Squadron Commander and officially became our Commanding Officer. Also, Art Whealy, who had left us in May to go to 9 Naval Squadron, had returned and he took over 'C' Flight during Armstrong's absence on leave in Canada. I now became the Flight Commander of 'B' Flight, my pilots being Flight Lieutenants J.A. Glen, A.B. Ellwood, W.H. Chisam and Flight Sub-Lieutenant K.D. MacLeod.

We received wonderful hospitality and kindness during our two months at Walmer and made a host of friends, many of them being the VAD nurses at the Army hospital there. This hospital had been the country home of Sir Charles and Lady Sargant and their family who, on the outbreak of war, had offered it to the War Office as a hospital for the wounded. Lady Sargant was now the hospital's matron and she and Sir Charles, who was a judge in the High Courts of Justice, lived in a smaller house, close to the hospital. They and their daughters, Millicent and Janet, were most kind to us and in addition to attending parties at the hospital we were also welcomed in their temporary home.

Sometimes we had a dance in our mess to which we invited the VAD nurses and other friends.

Another Walmer family to whom we owed a great debt of gratitude was that of Mr and Mrs W.P. Matthews and their daughters Lesley and

Bobby. They lived in a beautiful home called The Old House with a lovely garden which was the pride of Mrs Matthews who was an expert gardener. I have many happy memories of parties at The Old House.

After the war Lesley married Aubrey Ellwood who later had a distinguished career in the Royal Air Force, especially during the Second World War when he became Senior Air Staff Officer in Coastal Command and later AOC in C, Bomber Command. Now Air Marshal Sir Aubrey Ellwood has retired, he and Lesley live in Somerset and I enjoy meeting them from time to time in their beautiful home near Crewkerne.

Walmer Castle was the official residence of the Lord Warden of the Cinque Ports and it was there that the then Lord Warden, Earl Beauchamp, and Countess Beauchamp, lived with their family. They too were most hospitable and kind to us.

It was Countess Beauchamp who, after the war, had erected on the site of the aerodrome a memorial in honour of fifteen officers of the RNAS and RAF who, after being stationed at Walmer aerodrome, gave their lives for their country during the war. On 7th August 1920 this memorial was unveiled by Air Commodore C.L. Lambe, and then followed its dedication by the Chaplain-in-Chief of the RAF. It stands there today, on the cliff top, facing out across the Downs, and bearing the names of those officers.

Two days after arriving at Walmer, I went home on fourteen days' leave during which I celebrated my 21st birthday, and it was not until I returned that I made my first local flight at Walmer.

Our flying activities consisted almost entirely of short local flights which are entered in my Log Book as 'Practice Flights'. On only one occasion did we receive an Air Raid Alarm and that was in the early morning of 6th December. During the night I heard the drone of a twin-engined Gotha as it passed over Walmer and at 5 a.m. enemy raiders were reported over England and we were ordered to intercept them. We got dressed, proceeded to the aerodrome and took off just before dawn. I flew along the coast as far as the Isle of Sheppey climbing to 15,000 feet and when over Whitstable I saw ack-ack shells bursting at that same height but several hundred yards behind me. I turned in that direction thinking I might find a Gotha there but saw no sign of one and I concluded that the ack-ack gunners must have been firing at me. I returned to Walmer after patrolling for just under two hours and learned that the other pilots on the patrol had been equally unsuccessful.

Just before Christmas Lloyd Breadner led the whole squadron on a formation practice flight in which we flew low down over the countryside of Kent. This flight was in preparation for Christmas Day when, at eleven o'clock in the morning he again took the whole squadron in formation low over and around the hospital. The hospital staff knew about this display and many of the nurses and patients watched it from the terrace, many of the latter being in wheeled chairs.

The fly-past lasted about forty minutes and we afterwards walked over to the hospital and helped the nursing staff to wait on the patients at their Christmas dinner before returning to our own mess. In the evening we attended a concert in the hospital at the end of which Louis Bawlf, dressed up as Father Christmas, distributed presents from the Christmas Tree to all the patients. Christmas 1917 was greatly enjoyed by us all.

On Boxing Day Harold Ireland and I went to London by train on our way to Lincoln where we were to collect two Sopwith Camels, built by Clayton and Shuttleworth, from the Acceptance Park. These we were to deliver to RNAS Dover. We stayed overnight in London and the following morning continued our journey by train to Lincoln and arrived at the Acceptance Park in time for some lunch. Afterwards we collected our Camels and took off. We had no maps and knowing the compasses in our machines were far from accurate we decided to follow the railway line towards London until we saw that vast metropolis looming up ahead of us, when we would cross the River Thames to the east and over its estuary and follow the coast to Dover. All went well until we reached a large town, which I think was Peterborough, and from here railway lines branched off in more than one direction. I picked what I thought was the main line south but it turned out to be one heading well to the west of London.

Shortly before dusk we found ourselves heading towards the Chiltern Hills so I decided to land in a field just outside the village of Chinnor. I got down safely and was followed by Ireland who unfortunately broke his tail skid. The farmer in whose field we had landed came along and offered to put us up for the night. So after making arrangements with the RFC depot at Abingdon to guard the machines during the night, we had a meal with him at the farmhouse.

A charming local lady invited us to visit her during the evening so we went along to her very pleasant home and for an hour or two had an interesting conversation with her. She had lived for some years in Far East Asia and much of her furniture and ornaments came from there. I was intrigued by all this but had the feeling that there was something rather mysterious about both her and her home.

The following morning two RFC mechanics arrived from Abingdon and fitted a new tail skid to Ireland's Camel. One of them then started up my engine and I took off and circled around for a time waiting for Ireland to follow but he had some difficulty in getting his engine started and I did not see him again until I arrived back at Walmer. I flew to the RFC aerodrome at Port Meadow near Oxford, expecting Ireland to do the same, but he apparently decided to fly straight to Walmer. There was to be a farewell dance there at the end of the month and he had promised his VAD girlfriend that he would be there.

From Port Meadow an RFC pilot, Captain Norris, took me into Oxford by car and we had lunch together at the Randolph Hotel where I stayed the night. The following day the weather was too bad for flying so I went by train to my home in Enfield, returning to Port Meadow on New Year's Eve. I left there after lunch but had to land at the RFC aerodrome at Northolt as the weather was deteriorating with a lot of mist and failing light. I obtained permission to go up to London where I met some of my family and we went to see a show at one of the theatres before returning home for the night.

On New Year's Day I left Northolt in the afternoon hoping to reach Dover before dusk but again I ran into bad weather and landed at the RNAS Eastchurch where I stayed overnight. The following morning I took off from Eastchurch and finally landed at Dover about ten o'clock. When I reported to the Station Commander, Wing Commander Osmond, and handed over the Camel he remarked that it had taken me a long time to come from Lincoln but he seemed satisfied when I told him of the frustrating weather I had experienced throughout the trip.

I returned to Walmer in a Sopwith 1½-strutter flown by Flight Lieutenant Lusby, an old friend from when we were training together at Cranwell in 1916.

On arrival there I discovered that we were due to return to France that very day and that 4 Naval Squadron had already arrived from France to take over from us. In great haste I packed up my kit and in the afternoon we made an attempt to leave Walmer for Bray Dunes. However, as most of the ground staff had already left by sea from Dover, we only had a few mechanics remaining to start up our machines. Thus, only two Camels were ready to go before it became dark and misty so Breadner decided to postpone our departure until the following day. Some of the VAD girls had come up from the hospital to see us off to France and they were delighted to hear we were to spend another night in Walmer. One of them almost put her foot through the bottom plane of my Camel when she was investigating the cockpit.

We finally got away after breakfast, on the following morning and after dodging snow storms all the way across the Channel we landed at Bray Dunes forty minutes later. The fun and social life of Walmer were over and we were now to settle down again to the serious side of the war.

Before we returned to France from Walmer, awards of the DSC had been made to Armstrong, Beamish and Hayne. All three had been with the squadron for about one year and well deserved the award for all the splendid work they had done.

Our Records Officer, C.H. Nelson, about now, was replaced by Flight Lieutenant Frank Dudley Taylor, a portly chap of considerable intelligence. He became a very good friend of mine and remained so in the years between the wars. Like myself he rejoined the RAF during the last war during which we met from time to time. Dudley spoke several languages fluently including French and from certain remarks in our conversations I suspected he had been a secret agent and had landed behind the enemy lines on more than one occasion. These talks took place between the wars and I never pressed him to enlarge on the little he said, appreciating that secret agents thought it unwise and, indeed, disliked to talk about their experiences.

Freddie Armstrong returned to the squadron from his leave in Canada, soon after we arrived in France, and again took command of 'C' Flight.

The great battles of 1917, terminating in the battle of Cambrai towards the end of that year, were now over. Little or no advantage had been gained by either side and during the first two and a half months of 1918 there was a lull in the fighting during which the German High Command, owing to the desperate economic situation within the Fatherland, were ordered to prepare a final gigantic offensive against the Allied Armies, the objective being their complete and final defeat.

On 4th January at 2 p.m. I led my Flight on a high OP. We climbed to 14,000 feet and searched the sky but saw no EA before returning to Bray Dunes. This was my last patrol on Camel B3798 for on the morning of 6th January I took over the CO's aeroplane, B6401, and led my Flight on a Fleet Protective Patrol. We found the ships 20 miles off Ostend and gradually descending from 12,000 feet in wide circles scanned the area for EA. None were seen before we completed the patrol.

Routine daily patrols were carried out but it was not until the 22nd January that any EA were engaged. During the morning on that day I took up B6401 to test the guns which had been giving me trouble and, when at 12,000 feet, I saw a DFW two-seater east of Nieuport. I attacked and drove him down but eventually lost him in the clouds. I was still having trouble with the left-hand gun jamming and after landing handed over to the armourers for further attention. A second test in the afternoon proved satisfactory.

On this same day three of our Camels from another Flight picked up the ships off Nieuport and escorted them to Dunkirk. A formation of six EA was observed about this time to the north of Blankenberghe and were attacked but without decisive results whereupon an enemy destroyer opened fire on our Camels.

While the squadron was at Walmer Lloyd Breadner's wife, who had arrived in England from Canada, became a VAD nurse at the hospital there. Not unnaturally, Breadner applied for a posting to Home Establishment and the application being approved he left 3 Naval on the 23rd January. Breadner had served in 3 Naval since its formation in late 1916 and had shot down 10 EA and been awarded the DSC. His most memorable victory was that over the Gotha bomber which he forced to land in a field near the British GHQ on St George's Day 1917. After the war he became a prominent figure in the Royal Canadian Air Force as its Chief of Air Staff and in the latter part of World War Two its Commander-in-Chief in Europe. He retired as an Air Marshal.

Our new CO was Squadron Commander Raymond Collishaw DSO DSC, who had left 3 Naval in March 1917 to go into hospital with a badly frost-bitten face and was later posted to 10 (Naval) Squadron then equipped with Sopwith Triplanes. He had by now shot down 40 EA of which he claimed 33 when leading his famous 'B' Flight of 10 Naval in the summer of 1917.

Additional to these activities on 23rd January, eight Camels from 'A' and 'C' Flights carried out an OP south of Ostend-Thourout-Roulers. When over Houthulst Forest they met a formation of four DFWs and three new type scouts and a general engagement took place during which Anderson attacked and drove down out of control one of the

DFWs and several indecisive combats took place. Flight Sub-Lieutenant Youens in Camel B7184 failed to return and was reported to be a POW at a later date. His conqueror is thought to have been Leutnant Carl Degelow of Jasta 7 who later became a high-scoring German 'ace' and commander of Jasta 40. He was also the last recipient, in November 1918, of the Pour le Mérite Order.

During the morning patrol of 28th January when leading 'B' Flight and accompanied by three Camels of 'A' Flight, I observed below us two DFW two-seaters at about 10,000 feet above the Houthulst Forest. With Glen and Devereux I attacked one of them, firing at point-blank range. The observer was either killed or wounded and the engine hit as the propeller ceased to revolve. Flight Lieutenant Hayne reported seeing this EA going down in a spin. Other EA were also encountered on this OP near Roulers.

MacLeod attacked one and after he had fired a burst of 100 rounds it slipped into a spin and was still spinning at about 2,000 feet, though MacLeod was unable to see the final result. I attacked another DFW but without any decisive result.

On the following day Armstrong, leading 'C' Flight, saw five Albatros Scouts above him near Roulers so he continued to climb and eventually got above the enemy formation. Then the whole Flight dived on the EA and he fired about 200 rounds into one of them which turned on its back and fell in a spin. While watching it go down Armstrong was attacked by another EA which prevented him seeing whether it crashed although he felt certain the EA was out of control.

On 30th January I led 'B' Flight on an OP over the Ypres-Roulers-Dixmude area and when at 17,000 feet saw six Albatros Scouts about 2,000 feet below us near Gheluvelt. We attacked and Glen, Ellwood and myself shot down two of them out of control.

About this time Dudley Taylor demonstrated his useful ability as a scrounger. Whenever anything was required which could not be obtained through the 'usual channels' he seemed to know where to get it. Our pressing problem at the time was how to cope with the ground in our camp which was very wet and muddy.

A short distance away was an unoccupied RNAS camp with various equipment stored in its Bessoneaux hangars. Dudley Taylor discovered that one hangar was filled with duckboards so he got permission from the CO to take a lorry and bring back a load of these. They were the very things we needed and as soon as they arrived were unloaded and laid down to give us a clean walk between the various camp buildings.

Not long after this the once empty camp became occupied and a certain Flight Lieutenant from Dunkirk was put in charge of it. One morning he was invited to lunch in our mess, saw our duckboards and thought them just the thing for his own muddy camp. Dudley offered to sell him as many as he liked for five francs each. The deal was clinched and a day or so later Dudley took a lorry to the Bessoneaux hangar, loaded it up with duckboards and then drove it to the Flight Lieutenant's office, who saw it unloaded and happily paid over the money. Little did he realise that he was paying for his own duckboards! That money was a very useful contribution to the mess funds and enabled us to have one or two very good parties!

Dudley Taylor next had his attention drawn to an empty French camp at Adinkerke only a mile or so from Bray Dunes. He noticed that inside this camp was a very nice wooden hut, eminently suitable for our CO's office. So one night he took a lorry and a gang of ratings to the entrance of the French camp where a sentry was on guard. Dudley spoke to him and perhaps slipped him a few francs and the lorry with the ratings was allowed to pass into the camp while Dudley remained and conversed with him in his fluent French. The gang of ratings soon dismantled the hut, loaded it on the lorry, picked up Dudley at the gate and returned to Bray Dunes, the French sentry being quite unaware of the lorry's contents.

Late on the morning of 2nd February, Harry Chisam and I took off on a Hostile Aircraft Patrol (HAP) to intercept an enemy reconnaissance machine. At 20,000 feet we saw an LVG two-seater to the east of us and just west of Nieuport. We chased him beyond Middelkerke in the course of our attack and finally drove him down, though apparently under control. Unfortunately both Chisam and myself had a lot of trouble with our guns jamming otherwise I feel certain we would have shot him down.

Soon after this I flew with my Flight to Berck-sur-Mer where the RFC had organised a series of weekly courses in gunnery in the air and on the ground. The tests in the air were of two types and consisted of diving and firing on a floating target in a pond and firing at a canvas drogue towed by a BE2c. At my first attempt on the pond target I had 17 hits out of 200 possible and at a second attempt 15 hits out of 120 possible. On the towed target my one and only attempt produced 18 outers and 7 inners out of a possible 400. These were not very good results and I seem to remember that the efforts of some of my pilots were very much better.

Considering the vital importance to us of air-gunnery at the time, it is surprising – in retrospect – that neither we nor the authorities made much effort to improve the standard which was obviously inadequate, especially amongst the newly-trained pilots.

The results of the Berck-sur-Mer course were, indeed, so bad that I made an analysis of my combat claims and found that about two-thirds produced no definite result. Several other pilots of our squadron, all with good fighting records, confirmed this ratio as about correct for them, too.

These astonishingly poor results were the inevitable outcome of the omission – until late in WWI – from the gunnery syllabus of useful tuition and practice opportunities both during and after the training period. I can find no evidence in my own case of ever having done fixed-gun air-to-air (or air-to-ground) shooting prior to joining 3 Naval. Nor do I recall any unit – including operational squadrons – in which tuition or encouragement was given to pilots in the interests of greater efficiency.

For some unaccountable reason the authorities always seemed to regard air-gunnery as one of the expendable subjects of a pilot's training. In late April 1918 Yvone Kirkpatrick – one of my pilots – supposedly passed the course at No 2 Auxiliary School of Aerial Gunnery, Turnberry though his Training Brigade Transfer Card was marked, 'Time spent in the air; Nil. Left prior to completion of course'. Another friend, Bill Lambert, did slightly worse, being despatched to No 24 Squadron in France from this same 'School' after only four days and without even seeing a gun, aeroplane or the aerodrome!

Clearly, pilots were expected to develop their own skills and methods in this most important facet of war flying so, realizing my low standard of marksmanship, I resorted to surprising the enemy and only firing at point-blank range – tactics I would have recommended to the majority of WWI fighter pilots.

A day or two after our return from Berck-sur-Mer some officers from a French escadrille visited our squadron to arrange with us an escort for one of their aeroplanes due to carry out a photographic-reconnaissance on the following day. The CO brought them into the mess for drinks and in the course of the conversation asked whether they had ever flown on the Champagne front. As they spoke very little English they misunderstood him and one of them replied, in French, 'No thank you, not at this time in the morning'!

During the morning of the following day I led 'B' Flight to the point of rendezvous with the French machine. We circled around at 15,000 feet for a considerable time but failed to find it. However, before returning to Bray Dunes, I saw a two-seater Albatros near the Houthulst Forest and this we attacked and drove down.

The CO rang up the French escadrille to find out what had happened to their reconnaissance machine and was told that it had reached the rendezvous early and had proceeded unescorted. Apparently, after completing its reconnaissance it engaged in a fight with some EA before returning home.

Also on 17th February 'C' Flight, while on an OP, encountered a formation of eight Albatros Scouts near Roulers and a number of combats took place. Art Whealy attacked one of the EA, diving on it and firing a burst at about 100 yards range after which the EA went down steeply out of control.

The following day 'C' Flight again carried out an OP and met about 27 EA over Thourout. Several engagements took place; Louis Bawlf dived on an EA and after firing about 50 rounds at close range it went down completely out of control; Harold Ireland also tackled an EA and fired about 100 rounds at 100 yards range but had to abandon the attack as he was attacked from above by another. Armstrong, the Flight Commander, also had indecisive combats with EA.

On 21st February when leading my flight on an OP, I observed about 20 EA coming towards the lines from the direction of Menin. I picked out an Albatros Scout and fired a burst of about 30 rounds at point-blank range. The EA heeled over to the right and, falling beneath me, I lost sight of him though I believe he was badly damaged and probably went down out of control.

The following day I went on leave to England and did not return until 8th March when I found the squadron had moved on 3rd March to Mont St Eloi and were attached to the 10th Wing RFC.

CHAPTER IX

MARCH AT MONT ST ELOI

In the weeks before 3 Naval left Bray Dunes, certain amusing and interesting events had taken place. During the lull in the fighting, the higher authorities thought it a good idea to get the troops to 'Dig for Victory' and so-called experts were sent to the various units. A signal was received by 3 Naval stating that an agricultural expert had been posted to it and that transport was to be sent to collect him from Dunkirk. Thinking the expert would be someone of considerable importance, the CO went to Dunkirk in his own car to meet him and discovered he was an Army private. The CO asked him what was his experience of agriculture and horticulture. His reply was, 'Nothing. All I knows is that the Sergeant said I was posted to that there 3 Naval Squadron.' All very amusing, but the CO thinking that he had better do something useful with him, put Freddie Armstrong in charge of the squadron 'smallholding'. Armstrong and the 'expert' drew a plan showing the plots on which the vegetables were to be grown. Unfortunately progress stopped there as a day or so later the 'expert' went into Dunkirk on his day off duty, got drunk and we never saw him again.

We were not yet finished however with experts as another signal announced that an engineering expert would be arriving on the squadron from the Admiralty. This time the CO sent a Crossley tender and driver to meet him in Dunkirk. He turned out to be a Wing Commander, no less, and a genuine expert on aero-engines who spent most of his time with us sorting out technical problems with our Engineer Officer, Hugh Nelson. One afternoon for a change, Dudley Taylor took him up near the front line, close to Nieuport. I heard he was glad to return to the comparative security of our mess.

The operation most frequently flown at this time was the Offensive Patrol, or OP, carried out above or beyond the front line. My own tactics for these no doubt differed from those of other formation leaders but I considered them to be the best if the objective was maximum success with minimum losses.

Immediately after take-off we formed up and headed towards the line at our best rate of climb. Whilst still climbing along the line, all pilots maintained a thorough search of the sky, especially above and below to the east so as to spot any EA as soon as possible. If these were sighted I made certain that we were above and, ideally, up-sun to them. Clouds, too, were used as cover from which to stalk the enemy. This positioning was important before initiating an attack which was made as a steep dive by the whole flight.

Fire was opened at about 100 yards range and continued, in bursts, until it was necessary to break away, left or right, and regain height and formation. In the case of a single two-seater target, if the first attacker missed a following member of the flight would tackle it, and so on.

On EA in numbers a formation attack was made, each pilot selecting a target amongst them. Following the initial engagement the flight would climb and reform without delay, ready for further attacks on any EA still about.

I always tried to avoid prolonged involvement in 'dog fights' there being no sense in relinquishing the advantages of superior height. Nor did I favour headlong charges by my formation into that of the enemy – particularly if they were in greater numbers.

Continual vigilance and the ability to rapidly see and identify other aeroplanes were constant requirements of all pilots. Let Ron Sykes quote an example of this which, in the event, was humorous but might well have been tragic.

'The 17th American Aero Squadron was formed in our Wing with, I think, our squadron American, Bill Goodnow, as one of the flight commanders. On one of their first patrols for which "203" did an unofficial escort someone in the "17th" failed to see a high bunch of EA and flew under them but a "dog fight" by "203" stopped the latter from diving on the "17th".

'After the show a couple of our Camels landed at their aerodrome where some excitement prevailed. One pilot complained that a "203" Camel had dived through their formation and dangerously close to him. He took some convincing that the Camel was, in fact, a Fokker, shot down by someone in our HOP!'

Their inexperience in air-fighting did not extend to the field of liquid refreshments, as Ron explains. 'I clearly remember going to the American Mess that evening with Tich. A six-foot barman loomed up and said, "What'll you have?"

"Mixed vermouth, please," replied Tich.

"Mixed with what?" said the barman, "Whisky or brandy?"'

Goodness knows what we finally drank.

Our new home, Mont St Eloi, was a few miles north-west of Arras and about 10 miles west of Vimy Ridge. The aerodrome was situated on the summit of a ridge and on the opposite side of the valley below were the ruins of an old church. In the valley a Canadian remount cavalry unit was based, who very kindly allowed our pilots the occasional use of a couple of their horses. We were now on the First Army Front and air activity was increasing daily.

On the 8th March Aubrey Ellwood with MacLeod and Devereux attacked an enemy two-seater which immediately dived eastwards but they continued the attack and a trail of yellow smoke was seen to come from it. This EA eventually crashed and burst into flames near Tortequennes.

I now took over a new Camel B7203 and flew it on a short test flight on 9th March. On the same day Glen and Adam went out in search of low flying EA and found a two-seater DFW near Henin-Lietard which they quickly shot down in flames.

The following day, when leading my flight on an OP, I had an indecisive combat with a DFW two-seater near Douai. Shortly afterwards we encountered near Lens a formation of about a dozen Albatros and the new Pfalz Scouts. Several indecisive combats took place, in most cases the EA breaking off the fight and diving steeply away eastwards. However in this encounter EA were shot down out of control by Ellwood and Chisam while at the same time Art Whealy, when leading 'C' Flight, shot down an EA scout which was seen to crash and Britnell got one out of control.

On 11th March Armstrong, with 'C' Flight on an OP, attacked an Albatros Scout and broke it up in the air over Drocourt.

Next day in the course of an OP with my flight at 18,000 feet, we saw two Albatros two-seaters near Douai. They must have been out on a photographic-reconnaissance. I dived on one of them, opening fire at close quarters, and he immediately went down out of control.

A fairly new type of German two-seater fighter with double tailplanes and rear cockpit close to that of the pilot was making more frequent appearances on the Western Front. It was known as the Hannover and on the morning of 16th March the flight and I, on an OP, saw three of these EA flying high above Gavrelle. We went for them and Ellwood, Glen and I shot one of them down in flames while a second was attacked by Harry Chisam and seen to crash by one of our artillery-observation posts.

While on an OP during the morning of 18th March and flying at 17,000 feet we saw near Haubourdin a Rumpler two-seater which we attacked but were unable to get to close range as he dived away and completely outpaced us.

The German Rumpler two-seater of this period was an excellent reconnaissance aeroplane with a splendid performance. Its ceiling exceeded 20,000 feet and at that height it was faster than most of our single-seat scouts. On sunny and clear afternoons we could usually see one flying at a great height on a photographic-reconnaissance sortie many miles behind the British lines.

Also on the 18th Hayne attacked an enemy two-seater firing about 100 rounds at point-blank range. The EA dived underneath him and was immediately attacked at close range by Berlyn who saw the observer collapse on his gun and the EA crash alongside some houses about a mile east of Henin-Lietard.

On 19th and 20th March rain and low cloud prevented flying and at dawn on the 21st it was foggy. Under cover of this fog the Germans launched their great offensive along the 5th and 3rd Army Fronts which were south of our aerodrome. After a terrific bombardment by their artillery, the German infantry attacked in overwhelming numbers and within a few days had broken through and advanced many miles in a push towards Amiens.

At 10.15 on the morning of 21st March I led my flight on an OP and we climbed to 17,000 feet. The fog had cleared and it was a sunny day but visibility was poor and it was difficult to see the ground through the haze. After flying for about an hour I saw below us a large number of EA, among them a red triplane, near Douai. We attacked them and picking out an Albatros Scout I opened fire at close range and he went down out of control. I then had two more combats with Albatros Scouts, both with indecisive results. Jimmy Glen had helped me to shoot down this Albatros Scout out of control and Armstrong, with 'C' Flight, got another one down in the same category. The presence of the red triplane among those EA seemed to indicate that it was von Richthofen out with his Circus.

In the late afternoon of that same day I led a formation of 'B' and 'A' Flights on an OP, flying along the lines at 17,000 feet. Near Vaulx we intercepted an Albatros two-seater. Poor chap, he had not a hope of escaping us and we fell on him like a pack of bloodthirsty foxhounds who had caught up with their prey. Nearly all of us took part in the attack and eventually the EA turned completely over and descended on its back in a flat spin until it hit the ground and was completely wrecked on our side of the lines.

After considering my Combat Report, the CO decided to try to salvage as much as possible of the wrecked EA. He and I with one or two others, including Chief Petty Officer Finch, set out in a Crossley tender. Until we had passed through Arras and on to the road to Bapaume we met very little traffic and all was relatively quiet. But as we proceeded towards Bapaume, the noise of gunfire noticeably increased and shells passed over us and exploded, on the west side of the road. A touch of humour was brought into the picture by CPO Finch who kept exclaiming, 'That's one of ours' and 'That's one of theirs'!

As darkness fell the road became more and more congested with military vehicles of every description. We moved forwards at a snail's pace and sometimes not at all. The bombardment continued though fortunately none of the shells hit the traffic on the road as far as we could see. But the state of chaos was so great that Collie decided that it was now quite impossible to reach the crashed Albatros and ordered our driver to return to Mont St Eloi. By the following morning reports had been received that the Germans had made a complete breakthrough and any possibility of reaching the crashed EA had vanished.

On the morning of 22nd March I was up again with my flight on an OP and when flying at 17,000 feet observed and attacked an Albatros Scout, firing at about 50 yards range. The EA went down slipping and diving steeply, finally crashing near Boursies. I later attacked another Albatros Scout but without decisive result. In this same encounter, Ellwood shot down out of control another EA. Also during that day Armstrong, leading 'C' Flight, got one of a formation of nine EA which crashed near the trenches within the enemy's artillery barrage. Of other pilots in 'C' Flight on this patrol, Whealy attacked an Albatros Scout which also fell in our lines, Pierce shot another down just inside the enemy's lines and Louis Bawlf scored one EA out of control.

This had been a day on which 3 Naval had engaged in a great deal of air-fighting on the battlefront and with six victories to its credit had played its part in the struggle that was raging.

The following day I stood by with Adam, ready to take off to attack enemy spotter two-seaters when reported to be operating on the front. In response to a call we first went up at 9.30 and climbed towards Armentières, reaching a height of 10,000 feet. East of Armentières I found a Rumpler two-seater and attacked it. The EA immediately dived eastwards and, as Rumplers usually did, easily outpaced us and disappeared from sight. We landed after a patrol lasting less than one hour but were off again at 10.45 in response to a second alarm and this time we drove down a DFW two-seater near Bauvin before returning home.

During the day other pilots in our squadron successfully attacked EA. Ellwood and MacLeod, when on an OP, together shot down a Pfalz Scout which crashed near Noreuil and Armstrong claimed another of the type which he followed to a low altitude and saw crash near Vaulx. Whealy also brought down a Pfalz Scout out of control.

In the evening of 24th March Armstrong and I led our flights on an OP and at 14,000 feet observed a mixed formation of Albatros and Pfalz Scouts near Beaumetz. I attacked one of the former and shot it down out of control. This was followed by indecisive combats with an Albatros and a Pfalz Scout. Chisam, too, got one of the latter out of control while 'C' Flight were similarly credited with one.

The crisis of the battle came the next day, 25th March. About 7.30 a.m. an observer of No 59 Squadron RFC had reported very large concentrations of German infantry just east of Bapaume and soon they were sweeping onwards. The enemy broke through and in some places advanced several miles without meeting any opposition. Soldiers controlling traffic at crossroads behind the front line were taken prisoner before they realised what was happening. Army Headquarters had no idea as to the latest enemy positions.

It was this situation that prompted the issuing of an order from RFC headquarters by Major General Salmond that all scout squadrons were to concentrate on locating and shooting up enemy troops from a low altitude. The squadron received orders to carry out this Special Mission in the area around Bapaume.

The sky was overcast with cloud base about 1,000 feet when I took off with my flight at 12.45. On reaching the appointed area we broke flight formation and proceeded to work independently. I flew eastwards at 500 feet searching the ground for enemy troops. I observed both German and British troops but everything was very confused and it was difficult to sort them out one from the other. I could hear the sound of rifles and machine-guns firing and noticed bullet holes appearing in my top and bottom planes.

Suddenly from out of the clouds a two-seater flew right across my bows and as he turned eastwards I got into a position close behind him. I was about to open fire when a bullet hit my main petrol tank. Thinking I was being attacked from behind, I turned quickly but could see no EA so the bullet must have been fired from the ground. Petrol fumes entered the cockpit, the engine spluttered and stopped and I thought my machine was about to catch fire. I cannot deny that I was frightened as I descended with the intention of landing near our troops. But I soon recovered my self-control and switched on to my auxiliary fuel tank. The engine started and I eased the machine out of its dive only fifty feet above the ground and headed westwards.

Remembering that the auxiliary tank held only enough petrol for about 15 minutes flight, I knew I would have to refuel at least twice before reaching Mont St Eloi. I first refuelled at Lavieville aerodrome, then took off again for Bertangles. Here I landed and taxied to the hangars of No 54 Squadron RFC. I reported to their CO, Major Reggie Maxwell MC, who had been in command of No 18 Squadron RFC early in 1917 when we used to escort their FE2bs. Having told him my story, I tried to contact Mont St Eloi and while waiting for my telephone call to get through was invited to lunch with 54 Squadron. Among the squadrons at Bertangles was 5 Naval, a two-seat bomber unit equipped with DH4s. They had arrived there on the previous day, the second move since the 21st. Among their flight commanders was my friend 'Pompey' Bartlett with whom I had a short chat during my enforced stay.

At last I was informed that there was little chance of telephoning to my squadron as many of the lines had been destroyed by enemy action and those left were blocked with important army calls.

My Camel had by now been refuelled and I decided to take off at once for Mont St Eloi. I landed there as the Daily Reports were about to leave the Squadron Office for Wing Headquarters. I had already been recorded as 'missing' so the despatch rider was held up until that entry had been deleted from the Casualty Report. Now I heard the sad news that Freddie Armstrong had been killed during the morning's low-flying Special Mission. The other pilots of his flight reported seeing his Camel go down in flames and crash near Ervillers.

Army, as we called him, was a tall, fair-haired Canadian from Toronto, one of those who came to 3 Naval from No 3 Wing, RNAS, in February 1917. He was an experienced Flight Commander who combined an aggressive spirit with intelligence and common-sense. Army's keen sense of humour was often expressed with a considerable amount of bawdiness. I remember one such occasion when we were all having a meal in the mess and Art Whealy felt it necessary to remind him that the Padre was present. His reply was overheard by the Padre, who immediately retorted, 'No, Army, I shouldn't do that.' Armstrong, who had been awarded the Croix de Guerre when with No 3 Wing and the DSC for his service with 3 Naval, was liked by us all and we felt his loss deeply.

For the few remaining days of March we continued to carry out these low-flying, shooting-up missions, interspersed with one or two OPs and escorts. These low-level missions were thoroughly disliked by most of us as one became a mere target to be shot at all the time and it was a matter of sheer luck whether one got hit or not. Nor was it always easy to identify German from British troops, and while this was being done one became even more vulnerable. My method was to take the flight to a height from which likely targets could be seen clearly, then to dive down on them firing off all ammunition as quickly as possible and, having made a mental note of the positions of all enemy troops and transport, return home.

On 26th March I led my flight on two Special Missions in the Grandcourt-Pys area. While on the afternoon mission Harry Chisam was wounded in the hand. After landing back at Mont St Eloi he was discharged to hospital and did not return to the squadron. In the morning I took the flight on an escort of DH4s of 18 Squadron while they carried out a reconnaissance between Quiéry-la-Motte and Provin.

The following day in both the morning and afternoon I was again attacking enemy troops around Albert and in the evening flew an escort for the DH4s. On these low-flying missions I saw, lying wrecked on the ground the many British and German aeroplanes which had been shot down. I also noticed that the church at Albert had finally been demolished by German shelling. Bearing in mind that the inhabitants of Albert had predicted the end of the war would be in sight when the gilded statue on the spire was finally dislodged, we might have taken this destruction as a good omen.

On March 28th German shells began bursting in our vicinity at Mont St Eloi and we were ordered to pack up at once and move to Treizennes, an aerodrome close to Aire. I landed there with my flight on completing an OP during the afternoon of that day.

On 31st March my flight carried out two OPs. Both proved quite uneventful and were our last patrols as No 3 (Naval) Squadron. At midnight the Royal Naval Service and the Royal Flying Corps each terminated its separate identity and amalgamated to become one Service – the Royal Air Force.

CHAPTER X

SPRING SORTIES WITH THE RAF

When I rose from my bunk – I mean camp-bed – on the morning of April 1st, I was Captain Rochford, Commanding 'B' Flight, No 203 Squadron, Royal Air Force.

By the end of March the German drive towards Amiens had slowed down and nearly halted. Haig had asked Pétain, the French Commander-in-Chief, to defend that city with increased French forces and Pétain undertook to reinforce the local French Commander, but at the same time instructed him to fall back, if necessary, to cover Paris. If this had happened the French and British armies would have been separated and the German High Command might well have gained the decision on which it had staked all.

A conference was held in Doullens on March 26th to decide issues of victory or defeat. It was attended by the French President Poincaré, Prime Minister Clemenceau and Lord Milner from the British Cabinet. The outcome was that the French General Ferdinand Foch was appointed Supreme Commander of all Allied Armies on the Western Front. He at once set to work to co-ordinate the actions not only of the Allied armies on the ground but also those of the British and French Air Forces.

As the German offensive slowed down so did the enemy activity in the air. Thus during the early days of April we were able to resume our normal flying patrols.

Towards the end of March an old friend, Flight Commander Robert Alexander Little, was posted to 3 (Naval) Squadron from England. He took over the command of 'C' Flight and immediately began to show his prowess as a fighter pilot. On 1st April, when he had become a

Captain RAF, he attacked the rear machine of a formation of Fokker triplanes and fired about 200 rounds into it at close-range. The triplane went into a steep dive, the left hand planes broke off and it was seen to crash about three miles east of Oppy.

On the same day I was informed that I had been awarded the DSC and after an uneventful OP during the morning, led my flight in the evening on an escort for 18 Squadron carrying out a reconnaissance. We encountered no EA but on our return from this patrol Adam was missing. None of us had noticed him leave our formation or being attacked but it was reported later that he had crashed and been killed near Loos on the German side of the lines. One of the last RNAS pilots to join the squadron, he had shown promise and had shot down in flames a DFW two-seater.

At 4.30 on 2nd April I took 'B' Flight out to protect a solitary Bristol Fighter which was carrying out an artillery shoot near Armentières. We climbed to 11,000 feet and kept in close touch with our charge for more than two hours until it had completed the shoot. No attempt was made by any EA to interfere with us or the Bristol. On 5th April news came through that Ellwood had been awarded the DSC.

On the 6th Little attacked a DFW two-seater which dived into the clouds and as it emerged from them he pursued it again, firing at very close-range. The EA stalled and was seen by the whole flight to fall in flames and crash near Lens. On the following day he and his flight were attacked by ten Fokker Triplanes one of which Little shot down completely out of control. It was lost to sight as it fell into the clouds but later was seen crashed about one mile south-west of Violaines.

Very little flying was possible on 9th April owing to mist and drizzling rain when, early in the morning, the Germans launched a big offensive thrust towards Hazebrouck between Bois Grenier and the La Bassée Canal this time against the British First and Second Armies. Once again we had to carry out low-level operations and our Camels were fitted with bomb-racks to carry four 20-lb Cooper bombs. In the afternoon I was out with my flight bombing and shooting up targets along the La Bassée Canal. Little's flight was also engaged at this same time and he, in conjunction with two of my pilots, Glen and Ellwood, attacked and shot down an Albatros two-seater which crashed near Givenchy.

The Portuguese 2nd Division was holding a line immediately in front of La Gorgue where No 208 Squadron were based. The enemy in overwhelming numbers attacked this Portuguese Division and forced it to retreat through La Gorgue to the very edge of the aerodrome. There was thick fog locally that April morning which made flying impossible and the CO, Major Draper, made the difficult and heart-rending decision to destroy all his aircraft rather than let them be captured by the enemy. Sixteen Bentley-engined Camels were destroyed by fire on the aerodrome and the squadron with its transport stores and equipment went by road through the fog to an aerodrome at Serny not very long before La Gorgue was completely overrun by enemy troops the same afternoon.

In spite of bad weather I was out with my flight at 6.30 on the morning of 10th April, bombing and shooting up enemy troops and transport. Having completed this trip we landed at Liettres (also known as Estrée Blanche) aerodrome to which we had been ordered to move. During the day the news came through that Whealy had been awarded the DSC.

The following day while on a low-flying mission, Little encountered three EA two-seaters and with his flight attacked them. They were in turn immediately attacked by six Albatros Scouts, one of which Little engaged and sent down in a spin. He followed it and finally saw it crash near Neuve Eglise. On the same day Whealy despatched an LVG two-seater close to the canal near Sailly-sur-Lys and Glen destroyed an Albatros two-seater in flames near Givenchy.

The 12th April brought fine weather with exceptionally good visibility and many low-flying sorties took place, our squadron dropping no less than 220 Cooper 25-lb bombs on enemy troops and transport.

Low clouds and mist restricted flying on 13th April but I took my flight on an early morning low-flying mission. We soon climbed above the mist but very shortly fog developed, blocking out the ground from sight apart from a few small gaps in the cloud. I led the way down through a gap but, as we went through, the fog thickened and we had to break formation. Only Glen managed to find our aerodrome and land safely. Ellwood, having decided to release his bombs in a field well behind the British lines, landed and crashed in a ploughed field.

I decided to land without dropping my bombs and, after dodging around the slag heaps in the Béthune coalmining area, I picked a field in which to do so. As I approached it into wind I could just see through the mist a row of trees along the far boundary. I found myself overshooting so opened the throttle and just cleared those trees. Round I went and once again found myself overshooting and having to make a third attempt. The fog was now so thick that I just had to make a landing on this attempt. Fortunately it was successful and my Camel came to rest only a few feet from the edge of a gravel pit about 50 feet deep. I got out of my Camel but by now could not even see the boundaries of the field through the fog. However, I heard transport moving along a road and walked in that direction to stop a lorry. I was given a lift to a nearby Army unit where I rang up the squadron and reported my whereabouts.

My other pilot, John Denison, had apparently crashed in a field near Pernes and was killed but a post-mortem disclosed that a bullet had entered his head before the crash. The only witness was a Frenchwoman living nearby who, when questioned, said she saw a Boche aeroplane attack Denison and shoot him down. I imagine this EA must also have lost his way in the fog as one rarely found them flying so far behind our lines.

John Denison was a delightful youngster, only eighteen years of age, who had only been with us a few weeks so that practically all his flying had been done on low-level flying missions. He had shown courage and enthusiasm and I am sure he would have become a very good fighter-pilot. He was buried in the military cemetery at Pernes.

'B' Flight carried out two more low-level operations in the afternoon of that day and the squadron dropped a total of 152 Cooper bombs.

In spite of the bad weather on the following day the squadron dropped another 36 Cooper bombs and during the morning I took 'B' Flight out to locate enemy positions around Bailleul. I have no doubt that our report was found to be useful as information about enemy locations at this time was very difficult to obtain and frequently non-existent. We flew at a maximum height of 500 feet.

The crisis in the German thrust towards Hazebrouck came on 12th April and in the morning of that day Sir Douglas Haig issued his famous 'Backs to the Wall' Order which impressed upon everyone the gravity of the situation. Addressed to all ranks of the British Army in France and Flanders, it pointed out that for three weeks the enemy had made terrific attacks with the objects of separating the British from the French, taking the Channel Ports and destroying the British Army. But he had made little progress towards these goals owing to the determined fighting and self-sacrifice of our troops for which Haig expressed his admiration. The French Army was now moving rapidly, and in great force, to our support and, with our backs to the wall, each one of us must fight to the end.

Our squadron continued the bombing and machine-gunning of enemy targets for several more days. Then, on 21st April, Little burst into action again. Leading his flight, he attacked the rear machine of a formation of twelve enemy scouts. This was a Pfalz Scout and Little watched it fall to 1,000 feet near Neuf Berquin, completely out of control. He was then attacked by six EA and his controls were shot away, causing his Camel to dive to within 100 feet of the ground, when it flattened out with a sudden jerk, breaking its fuselage below the pilot's seat. Little had by now unfastened his safety-belt and was thrown clear when the machine struck the ground. One EA continued firing at him, diving to within about 30 feet of the ground while Little replied with shots from his revolver.

Later that day we heard that Captain A.R. Brown had shot down the famous German 'ace' Manfred von Richthofen who crashed to his death behind our lines near Corbie. Roy Brown was a Canadian and a Flight Commander in No 209 Squadron.

In the evening of 21st April Barney Bawlf, the brother of Louis Bawlf, was killed. I had asked him to take two new pilots out on a formation practice flight and was watching him climb at about 1,000 feet when he suddenly stalled and spun into the ground not far from the aerodrome. His brother went with the ambulance to the scene of the crash but Barney died in it while on the way to the hospital. Louis never quite got over the loss of his young brother and I think this sad case raised doubts as to the wisdom of having two brothers flying in the same squadron.

Soon after breakfast on 22nd April I led my flight out on an offensive sweep and after dropping our bombs on enemy targets, we climbed to 12,000 feet and were attacked, over Merville, by 15 Albatros Scouts. A short, sharp engagement took place during which I had two indecisive combats. Whealy and 'C' Flight also encountered enemy scouts and attacked one with a burst of fire from about 50 yards range. The EA went down completely out of control and crashed near Merville.

On the morning of 25th April 'B' Flight was sent on a Special Mission to bomb La Gorgue and shoot up targets in the vicinity. We carried out this duty without opposition from EA and so made our contribution to the 52 bombs dropped by 203 Squadron that day. Before the end of the month Beamish, who had been away sick in hospital, returned to the squadron and Little went to England on leave. Also during those last days of April the German attack on our Front was halted and he turned his attention to the British and French armies further south.

Our own casualties, from the commencement of the German

Offensive on 21st March until the end of April, amounted to eight killed and two wounded. Two of those killed, Sands and Moyle, collided in mid-air and fell within the enemy lines.

Our work in the past weeks had consisted mainly of bombing and shooting-up ground targets from low altitude, much of the time in heavy rifle and machine-gun fire, and it was then that I experienced some mental and physical ill-effects besides noticing them in my fellow pilots.

These Special Missions – sometimes four or more in a day – imposed a much greater strain on one than did the Offensive Patrols. At the same time we lost more pilots, some, shortly after joining us, others being old friends who had served in the squadron for a year or more. The element of doubt as to the outcome of the German advance was also a cause of tension not to mention the unsettling, tedious and frequent moves to new aerodromes.

The cumulative effect of such strain depended upon the individual temperament, of course, but invariably those who best survived these pressures were those who, by nature, were calm and disinclined to panic reaction. All pilots were very tired after each day of intensive and dangerous low-flying straffing. However, it was the self-controlled and unruffled ones who managed to get a good night's sleep. And that made all the difference.

By the beginning of May we had discontinued our low-level bombing and machine-gun attacks and had returned to Offensive Patrols and Escorts duties along with Offensive Sweeps which were intended to clear the sky of EA at all heights and rarely lasted longer than 1½ hours. My flight carried out its first OS on the morning of 2nd May. It only lasted thirty minutes and no EA were encountered. Soon afterwards I flew over to Remaisnil to see my brother Bill who had been posted to No 70 Squadron, then equipped with Clerget Camels. I had lunch with him and the squadron before returning to Liettres. On 3rd May Aubrey Ellwood left us on being posted to the Air Ministry. He had been in 'B'

Flight since I took it over at Walmer and I was very sorry to lose him for he had shot down eight EA and was a pillar of strength to us.

EA were active all that day and Whealy attacked an EA two-seater, opening fire at about 150 yards range. It started to dive followed by Whealy who got within about 100 yards and gave it a long burst. The EA then went into a vertical dive and was seen to crash into a house about a mile from Lens. Enemy aeroplanes were also shot down, out of control, by Beamish and Hayne.

In the afternoon of 6th May I went off on a lone flight to look for any German reconnaissance two-seaters that might be about. Near Hazebrouck I saw an LVG flying at about 17,000 feet and chased after him. Unable to cut him off, I tried to overtake him and close the range but he was faster than me so I was forced to open fire at long-range. Even then I had trouble with my guns jamming and he was able to reach safety well behind his own lines.

There was considerable enemy activity in the air on 9th May and the squadron shot down three EA. Whealy attacked and shot down a Pfalz Scout which crashed east of Herlies, Beamish fired at close-range about 100 rounds into a Fokker triplane which was diving on one of our machines and Le Boutillier shot down one of a formation of triplanes which nose-dived and was seen to crash. I attacked and drove down a couple of DFW two-seaters over Pacaut Wood, one of them when I was out alone soon after lunch.

By mid-May 'B' Flight had become one of new pilots, the last of the old guard, Jimmy Glen, having been posted to England on 15th May to take up a job at Air Ministry. Jimmy was one of the Canadians who came to us from No 3 Wing, RNAS. He was quite a few years older than most of us and I was fortunate to have had such a splendid pair as he and Aubrey Ellwood to fly on either side of me when on patrols. In all Jimmy had shot down sixteen EA. He was engaged to the American actress Josephine Earl then appearing in *The Lilac Domino* at one of the London theatres. No doubt that was the reason for his getting posted to the Air Ministry in London! The pilots now in my flight were Kirkpatrick, Stone, Brown and Prideaux.

On 14th May Art Whealy, leading 'C' Flight, attacked an LVG two-seater which fell out of control and was seen to crash near Richebourg.

The following day when with my flight on an Offensive Sweep we attacked a DFW two-seater which Brown and I shot down out of control over Estaires. Whealy and Britnell found a DFW two-seater which they crashed near Pont du Hem. Meanwhile 'A' Flight encountered another two-seater, an LVG, and this stayed and put up a fight. All our pilots took part in the combat and eventually the EA crashed near La Bassée. One pilot who took part in the fight was Lieutenant W. Goodnow of the American Air Services; like many of the US pilots at this time attached to an RAF squadron for operational experience, Bill Goodnow had been posted to No 203 Squadron and flew with us for some time before being posted to an American squadron.

On 16th May not only did we move from Liettres to the aerodrome at Izel-le-Hameau but the squadron had a very successful day in the air and EA were shot down by Beamish, Breakey, Britnell, Le Boutillier and Whealy.

The following day while on an OS with my flight we ran into a large number of Pfalz Scouts near Estaires and a dog-fight took place. I had several indecisive combats but shot down one EA which crashed in a field near Beaupré. Another one was destroyed in flames by the flight. We lost Prideaux on this patrol but one of my pilots reported seeing him descending near Merville apparently under control. I hoped this report was correct, although it clashed with an impression I had – and retain even to this day – of a Camel going down on fire during this dog-fight.

Little had now returned from the UK and took command of the squadron while Collishaw was away on leave. On 17th May Beamish shot down an EA scout which crashed near Merville and Hayne, seeing a DFW two-seater approaching our lines, got behind it and attacked it from the east with two good bursts of fire before he was observed.

The EA dived steeply and Hayne continued to attack until, at about 4,000 feet, it stalled, side-slipped out of control and finally crashed near Steenwerke.

On 18th May the squadron claimed another four victories. Beamish and Breakey attacked a Rumpler two-seater which went into a steep nose-dive and burst into flames. Hayne, with 'A' Flight, saw ten Pfalz Scouts about to attack three Sopwith Dolphins so they tackled three of these EA one of which went down in a steep spiral, crashed and burst into flames between Merville and Estaires. Another Pfalz was driven down out of control by Hayne near Neuf Berquin. And Little added another victory to his big score by shooting down out of control a Pfalz Scout.

During the morning of 19th May I led 'B' Flight on a high OP, had an indecisive combat with a two-seater LVG and shot down a DFW two-seater out of control near Merville. On the same day Hayne attacked a Pfalz Scout head-on and after a burst at close range the EA nose-dived and crashed near Merville.

Having escorted DH4s of 205 Squadron late in the evening I decided to pay them a visit. So, soon after lunch on the following day I flew to their aerodrome at Bertangles. Pompey Bartlett had been posted to England for a rest but I met Major Goble, a one-time Flight Commander in 8 Naval Squadron when it was formed in 1916, who was now in command here. I was also introduced to a pilot named Monty Wright whose brothers had been at school with me before the war. I had tea with him and the other squadron officers before returning to Izel-le-Hameau. The same evening, about six o'clock, I led 'B' Flight on a Special Mission to bomb billets near Merville and shoot-up troops in front of Nieppe Forest. We completed the trip and were back home in just over one hour. Sixty minutes later we were sent out again to repeat the operations at the same places. Again we had no trouble and landed back at Izel-le-Hameau at eight o'clock.

At dawn on 21st May I had 'B' Flight on an OP and at 15,000 feet we saw below us a DFW two-seater. Berlyn and I attacked it and it eventually nose-dived and crashed near Neuf Berquin. While on patrol, the following day, Little had to return home owing to engine trouble after he had shot down an EA at Hemal Mory. Before reaching the lines he encountered an Albatros two-seater which he attacked at close-range and it crashed into a railway cutting at St Leger.

After an uneventful OP that morning, I flew over to Estrée Blanche in the afternoon for the purpose of testing the performance of my Bentley-engined Camel against the Clerget and Le Rhône versions. We made three runs over a measured mile course with the following results:

	1st	2nd	3rd
BR1 Camel	20.40 secs	25.60 secs	24 secs
Le Rhône Camel	20 secs	25.40 secs	25 secs
Clerget Camel	23.60 secs	29.80 secs	42.20 secs

I believe these results were extremely inaccurate as they were carried out with a stopwatch and not by modern electric timing. They can hardly be considered true comparisons of the speeds of the three Camels. For instance, the 20 seconds run by the Le Rhône Camel gave it a speed of 180 mph which was quite absurd even allowing for the fact that we were allowed to dive onto the starting point.

The climbing test turned out to be a farce. Each machine carried a sealed barograph but none of them worked. However, I checked my climb to 20,000 feet by the clock and the altimeter in the cockpit with the following result:

10,000 ft in 11 minutes
15,000 ft in 20 minutes
18,000 ft in 30 minutes
20,000 ft in 40 minutes

During this late period of May bombing raids at night were being carried out by the Germans behind the British front, mainly with medium-size twin-engined bombers. The attacks were made on a variety of targets, some of them many miles behind our lines. We often heard the droning of the engines of these bombers as they passed above our aerodrome on the way to or from their targets. Always spoiling for a fight, this was eventually more than the irrepressible Little could bear. Although '203' was not a night-flying squadron, Little decided to attack these enemy bombers on his own.

Not long after darkness had fallen on the night of 27th May, I was in the mess drinking and talking with other pilots of our squadron. We heard the engines of a German raider as it passed overhead. Little left the mess and soon afterwards the familiar sound of a Bentley rotary reached our ears from the direction of the aerodrome. The noise temporarily faded as the Camel taxied away from the hangars, then became louder as on full-throttle it took off into dark night. Later Kiwi Beamish came into the mess and confirmed that Little had gone up in his Camel – not for the first time – to attack the German bombers. Three hours passed by and there was still no sign of Little's return. His fuel supply must have been long since exhausted but no message had come through reporting his landing elsewhere.

After some hours had passed, Major Booker of No 201 Squadron telephoned to say that a Camel had been found completely wrecked near Noeux with the body of the dead pilot lying beside it. Booker had gone at once to the scene of the crash and identified the body as that of Little whom he knew well as they had been together in 8 Naval during 1917.

From the wrecked condition of his machine it seems probable that Little was either dead or unconscious at the moment of impact. At some time prior to this he had been wounded in the thigh by a single bullet. He was officially reported to have died from wounds and shock. The full story of Little's tragic last flight that night will never be known, but he must have been wounded by the return fire of a gunner when attacking an EA. Many years later Raymond Collishaw told me that he had made a thorough research of the activities of the German twin-engined bombers on that particular night in May 1918. None of these claimed to have encountered a British aircraft, but a German two-seater did in fact claim to have shot down a British aircraft at the appropriate time and place. Maybe that unknown two-seater's observer fired the fatal shots which so abruptly cut short the magnificent fighting career of this outstanding pilot.

Robert Alexander Little, one of the bravest men I have known, loved air fighting and was quite without fear. He came to England from Australia early in the war and learned to fly at one of the civilian flying schools at Hendon where he got his Royal Aero Club pilot's certificate on 27th October 1915.

At the time of his death Little had scored 47 victories, ten of these having been obtained in the two months he was with our squadron and during part of which period he was on leave in England. He was a deadly accurate marksman both in the air and on the ground and carried a revolver which he always took with him into the air. With it he practiced on rats around the camp. He was also, apparently, a very capable performer with a .22 sporting rifle as Ron Sykes recalls: 'Captain Little, my Flight Commander, aimed to be the fastest gun on the Western Front through regular practice with his 22 rifle! Walking with him round the aerodrome, looking for a target and not finding one, I threw my RN cap into the air like a clay-pigeon and said, "You can't hit that". But he did and my cap had that bullet-hole through it ever after.'

It has been said that Little sometimes hypnotised the pilots in his flight 'to make them brave' before going up on patrol but I find this difficult to believe and, as I knew all those pilots well, I can definitely say that none ever mentioned to me that this took place. I do remember one or two occasions in the mess when Little pretended to hypnotise a pilot but I always considered this to be an amusing joke on his part.

Above: 'Kiwi' Beamish, after losing a wheel on take-off, crashed his Camel ('Tiki', N6377) when landing back at Bray Dunes.
Right: Forward view from a Sopwith Camel cockpit.
Below: The unveiling ceremony of the memorial to RNAS pilots at Walmer aerodrome. In the foreground are the widow and son of R.A. Little.

...osite top: When based ...Calmer some pilots of 3 ...al took advantage of the ...xed discipline to paint ...heir Camels in a variety ...nusual and bizarre ...mes.

...osite middle: Officers of ...3 Squadron RNAS, Bray ...es, February 1918. The ...or is fourth from left in ...middle row.

...osite bottom: ...Sopwith Camels of ...aval at Bray Dunes, ...uary–February 1918.

...t top: Sopwith Camel ...n by the author during ...uary–February 1918 on ...rations from Bray Dunes.

...t middle: A Sopwith ...el of 3 Naval/203 ...which fell into enemy ...ds. Otto Kissenberth, a ...d German fighter pilot, ...id to have later flown ...combat against Allied ...ts.

...w: On March 10th ...8, K.D. Campbell of 3 ...al was forced to land ...nd the German lines ...re this photograph of ...Camel (B7230) was ...n.

Above: The author (right) and Lt Stone, No 203
Squadron RAF, April 1918. Stone was later killed in
action when serving with No 201 Squadron.
Below left: Robert A. Little.
Below right: Major Raymond Collishaw.

Above: Pilots of No 203 Squadron RAF, Izel-le-Hameau, pause to remember a fallen comrade, R.A. Little. Left to right: L. Bawlf, A.T. Whealy, H.F. Beamish, Major Collishaw, the author.
Below: A cheerful group of pilots of 3 Naval photographed at Estrée Blanche in early 1918. Left to right: E. Pierce, E.T. Hayne, A.T. Whealy, H.F. Beamish.

Opposite top: The squadron's living quarters at Izel-le-Hameau, 1918.
Opposite middle: The Sopwith Camels of No 203 Squadron RAF, lined up at Izel-le-Hameau on July 8th 1918. The nearest machine was successively flown by Major Collishaw, the author and Major T.F. Hazell.
Opposite bottom, left to right: Ron Sykes; O.C. Le Boutillier; W.W. Goodnow, USAS.
Right: S.W. Rochford – the author's brother Bill.
Below: HM King George V talks to the author whilst inspecting No 203 Squadron at Izel-le-Hameau, August 8th 1918. 'Waacall' was the Sopwith Camel (D9618) flown by the author at that time.

Above: A late casualty in No 203 Squadron was Lt H.W. Skinner who crashed at Morenchies after being severely wounded in combat on October 2nd 1918.
Right: Major T.F. Hazell.
Below: Tich Rochford and Mrs Kirkpatrick, wife of a squadron colleague of 1918.

Great fighter pilot though he was – he won the DSO and bar, the DSC and bar and the Croix de Guerre – Little had another side to his character which was not of war. He loved nature and had a small flower garden close to his hut. His remarkable eyesight and powers of observation would be demonstrated if one took a walk with him in the countryside. He could pick out animal trails that his companion had missed. This information was given to me by the Canadian E.R. Grange who was Little's close friend and flew with him in 8 (Naval) Squadron. By his death, we in 203 Squadron lost a friend whom we liked and admired.

Hayne shot down an Albatros Scout to mark the end of May. Early in June, when out on a Special Mission, I attacked an LVG two-seater and sent it down out of control near La Bassée. Two days later when leading 'B' Flight on an OP we encountered a flight of Fokker triplanes. I attacked and got one of them down out of control near Neuve Eglise and also had an indecisive scrap with a similar type near Armentières. Whealy, with 'C' Flight, also shot down out of control a triplane near Lestrem.

On the following day, 8th June, I departed for England on leave and before returning to France attended an investiture at Buckingham Palace to receive the DSC and Bar from King George V. I also saw two or three shows at the London theatres. One of these was the musical comedy *Going Up*. The amusing story was centred around a farcical aviation theme and featured a French aviator, a challenge to an air-race and a comedian-hero who did not know one end of an aeroplane from the other but triumphed in the end. Amongst the 'props' wheeled onto the stage was an actual aeroplane of well-known type. Imagine my surprise, therefore, when one of the actors in the scene spoke the line, 'Ere, that's one o' them *Whitehead* planes, ain't it?'

Indeed, it was not, being a genuine Sopwith Pup, but I had to chuckle over this ingenious advertising ploy by the Whitehead company who were then building under licence aircraft of Sopwith design.

I remember that amongst the stars in this show were Joe Coyne and Evelyn Laye, a beautiful and talented young actress of eighteen, whose fame was to increase during her career in the many years ahead.

While I was on leave Raymond Collishaw resumed operational flying. He took over my Camel D3417 and had the aperture in the centre-section enlarged to give a wider view of the sky above. Having been tied to squadron administrative work for several months he was now able to get back to air-fighting which was much more to his liking. On 11th June Collishaw at the head of 'B' Flight led the whole squadron on an OP during which he shot down two Pfalz Scouts, one crashed and the other out of control. Before the end of the month while on Special Missions alone he shot down two Fokker D.VIIs which crashed and a Pfalz Scout which went down out of control.

We enjoyed a little light relief about this period through the occasional visits of Harry Ford, one of the characters of the RNAS/RAF and subject of many anecdotes. He was already friendly with our Canadians – especially Collie – having trained with them at Redcar but his piloting career was cut short through a disabling leg injury sustained when a crate of beer he was fetching for No 2 Wing's mess broke adrift in the cockpit of his Avro!

With the need for new aerodromes to be rapidly set up in France in 1918, Harry – now a Major, RAF – was in charge of this operation, hence his nickname, 'Bessoneaux Bill'. He called in one day to see Collie who was away. On being told this, Harry studied his watch intently for quite a time then suddenly said, 'Tell him I'll be back next week'.

On a visit to London in 1918 Collishaw met Harry who, characteristically, had taken French leave to attend a race-meeting. The rest of the tale, related by Collie, was typical. At the conclusion of some business with a tailor in the Strand, Harry invited the latter out for a drink. The man hesitated, but, indicating a waiting customer in the shop, Harry said, loudly, 'I'm sure this gentleman would look after the place until you return'. Looking somewhat nonplussed, the gentleman, nevertheless, sportingly agreed to do so.

As the unwilling guest was being propelled towards an adjacent bar he was heard to ask Harry, 'I suppose, sir, you do realize that the gentleman *you* left looking after my shop is the Secretary of War, Lord Derby?'

I returned from leave on the last day of June and found that our American pilot Weston Goodnow had left us on posting to the 17th American Aero Squadron. During the short time he was with us he had shot down two EA both of which crashed. We were very sorry to lose him.

By about the beginning of June 203 Squadron had returned to its normal flying of Offensive Patrols. Enemy activity in the air had not been very great and only fourteen EA were shot down during the month.

CHAPTER XI

A SECOND SUMMER OF STRIFE

The United States troops had now arrived on the Western Front in large numbers and July was a month of preparation for the Allied counter-attack and final assault on the German armies. The 4th July, being American Independence Day, Collishaw invited several American and Canadian officers to our mess for drinks. When the time arrived for them to leave us, many were in such a state that few of them could remember from where they came. So Collishaw put them all in a Crossley tender and he himself sat in front with the driver; he ordered the driver to stop at various camps, fetched out the Officer of the Guard and asked him whether any of these drunken officers belonged to his unit. Eventually all were safely delivered to their respective units.

Earlier in the day Collishaw had gone out alone to look for EA. He found two DFW two-seaters near Dixmude and attacked them. In trying to evade his attack the DFWs collided in mid-air and both crashed behind their own lines. On the following day Dixie, our South African pilot, while out on an OP, successfully attacked a Fokker biplane and it crashed near Ypres. On the same patrol Fricker shot down a Fokker D.VII out of control.

A few days later Whealy, while leading his flight on an OP, attacked a Fokker D.VII which crashed near Farbus.

During the following two weeks air activity was very slight on our front and it was during this period that Collishaw made plans for me to go out with him one morning, just before dawn, to attack a German aerodrome in the Douai area. He gave me no actual date but said it would be in the near future and we discussed details for this operation.

On 20th July I was leading my flight on an OP when we saw a

DFW two-seater. Sidebottom and myself attacked and it crashed near Lestrem. On the same patrol, Rudge, a new pilot in my flight, tackled an LVG two-seater which crashed near Merville. Collishaw was again out alone and shot down another DFW two-seater and this too crashed near Merville. He then also attacked a DFW which fell out of control over Miraumont.

During the evening of 21st July I walked over to No 64 Squadron and spent a pleasant hour or two drinking and having a quiet chat with a friend of mine, Jimmy Slater, one of their flight commanders. Eventually I returned to my bunk and went to bed about midnight. I soon fell asleep.

At 3 o'clock I was awakened by a knock on the door and Collishaw entered the room followed by a sentry carrying a hurricane lamp. Collishaw told me the day had now arrived for our dawn attack on Dorignies, an aerodrome near Douai. As I had managed only three hours' in bed since my evening with Jimmy Slater I felt much more like continuing my sleep than going out to attack a German aerodrome. However, I pulled myself together, got up and dressed and joined Collishaw in the mess where we had some tea and biscuits. I was then feeling much better. We walked together to the aerodrome where our Camels were all ready, standing side-by-side outside the hangar.

Engines were run up to maximum revs; then just before the break of dawn Collishaw took off and I followed soon afterwards. It was a beautiful morning with a cloudless sky and as I climbed the dawn rose above the horizon, lighting up the eastern sky. Its rays were reflected by the waters of the River Scarpe and the Lens-La Bassée Canal, gradually shedding light with a kaleidoscopic effect over the whole countryside. It was a lovely sight to contemplate and momentarily I almost forgot the purpose of my mission. But there was no time to waste as I wanted to get the attack on Dorignies completed before the German scouts had time to get into the air and intervene. So far I had not been fired at by German Archie nor had I seen any other aircraft in the sky.

Now, at 5,000 feet, I saw below me Dorignies. I throttled back my engine and dived down towards the target reaching a speed of more than 150 mph. At about 200 feet I attacked the buildings and hangars, firing all my ammunition into them and dropping three bombs on the living quarters and a fourth on a hangar which caught on fire. I then flew off westwards at a low height, opening the throttle so that the engine ran at 1,200 rpm, the safe maximum revs for a Bentley rotary if one wished to avoid trouble from cracked pistons or cylinders. I soon crossed the lines and landed safely back at Izel-le-Hameau.

Not long afterwards Collishaw also landed. He had waited up above until I had completed my attack which undoubtedly stirred things up at Dorignies. He then attacked with machine-gun fire three aeroplanes which were being brought out of a hangar, and dropped his four bombs onto the camp buildings from a height of 150 feet. Before returning home he attacked, at 800 feet, a two-seater which was about to land on the aerodrome and it fell in flames. Two hours after landing at Izel-le-Hameau Collishaw returned to Dorignies to see what damage had been done by our strafe. He was attacked by three Albatros Scouts, one of which he shot down and saw crash.

After having a good breakfast I led my flight on an OP at nine o'clock. We climbed to 17,000 feet and saw below us an Armstrong-Whitworth two-seater being molested by two Fokker D.VIIs. We quickly dived to the aid of the Big Ack and, attacking one of the Fokkers, shot it down out of control. The other one was destroyed by the observer in the Armstrong-Whitworth which had put up a wonderful performance when evading these two EA.

We now started to climb again and, when at 9,000 feet, I saw in the distance, well to the east of the lines, another patrol of five Fokker biplanes. I decided to continue climbing as quickly as possible, to try to get above them and, if possible, between them and the sun. At last, at 17,000 feet, we were in this advantageous position. Unfortunately, our numbers had been reduced to four as Kirkpatrick had been unable to keep in the formation owing to engine trouble.

A SECOND SUMMER OF THE CAMELS

Over Carvin I decided to attack the EA and dived steeply onto them. Picking my Fokker, I held my fire until I was almost colliding with him. I got off one short burst and he fell out of control. Sidebottom shot down a second which was seen to crash, and a third one fell out of control after being attacked by Stone. I saw Rudge attack a fourth, which went down in flames. We lost sight of the remaining Fokker, after he had broken off the fight and dived away eastwards. When we resumed formation to return home, I noticed one Camel was missing and after landing at Izel-le-Hameau discovered the missing pilot was Rudge. None of us had seen him go, but later the Germans reported he had been shot down and killed.

Arthur Rudge, who had been a fellow pupil at my preparatory school, joined 203 Squadron from 66 Squadron. They had been transferred from France to the Italian Front where air activity was much less intensive than that on the Western Front in France. Pilots, therefore, could roam about deep behind the enemy lines with little risk of being attacked by overwhelming numbers of EA. I suspect he had wandered a long way over the lines during our fight with the Fokkers. He was a brave lad who during his short time with us had destroyed two EA and had demonstrated his courage in a scrap he had with the LVG two-seater on 20th July. He drove the EA down to 2,000 feet well behind the lines whereupon the German pilot started to circle round a hospital marked with a red cross. Rudge got quite close to the LVG and gave it a burst of fire from the side, observing his tracers raking the fuselage from the cockpit to the tail. The EA turned onto its back and what appeared to be the observer's map case fell out followed by the observer himself. Then the machine with the pilot still in it continued its descent and finally crashed upside down in a canal.

I led my flight on an OP at 6.30 on the morning of 25th July and at 12,000 feet we encountered two Fokker D.VIIs near La Bassée. We attacked them and I shot down one and Sidebottom the other, both being seen to crash. Unfortunately Brown failed to return from this patrol and although one of my pilots thought he saw him descend under control, the Germans later reported Brown as killed.

On the evening of 31st July a very good Canadian concert party called 'The Red Hackles' visited us and put on a show in our theatre, a Bessonneau hangar. About halfway through the show, when it was dark, German bombers came over and dropped one or two bombs nearby which did no damage. After the show when we were all back in the mess, drinking and singing round the piano, the bombers were over again. This time a stick of bombs dropped right across our camp, straddling the Officers' Mess. The blast shook the building, bringing down pictures from the walls and smashing glasses in the bar. Bomb splinters pierced the walls of the wooden building, wounding Kirkpatrick in the arm, Lick in the head and Towell, our Equipment Officer, in the leg. Smith, one of our batmen, who was standing outside the door of a hut, was hit in the mouth by a small piece of shrapnel. All were sent away to hospital in the ambulance, where poor Smith died a few days later.

Having dealt with the wounded, Collishaw and two or three of us walked up towards the aerodrome to make a further check-up. Lying dead in the roadway behind the hangars we found the body of one of the concert party with a gaping wound in his back, a bomb having landed only a few yards from him. Later, Collishaw, Whealy and I proceeded to one of the machine-gun posts on the aerodrome where we remained in case more bombers should attack the camp.

Soon afterwards a bomber flew over the eastern boundary of the aerodrome and dropped bombs among the buildings of No 13 Squadron. One bomb scored a direct hit on a hut in which airmen were sleeping. Collishaw left Whealy and myself in the machine-gun pit and walked across the aerodrome to 13 Squadron where he found nearly all the men in the bombed hut had been killed or badly wounded. He stayed to organise the transfer of the wounded to hospital.

There was another fatality in our squadron during the afternoon of this day. Some of our airmen were playing an impromptu game of cricket out on the aerodrome when a new pilot taxied out in a Camel and proceeded to take off. Without apparently noticing it, he steered straight towards some of the players on the pitch who scattered and all but one of them got clear. The unfortunate victim was struck by the propeller and killed instantly and the aeroplane was badly damaged in the subsequent crash. The pilot sustained injuries and shock and was taken away to hospital.

During the last week of July we began to carry four bombs on every OP and these we dropped from low height on the enemy opposing the Canadian Corps before climbing to continue our OP. This bombing continued through the first week of August during which there was not a great deal of enemy air activity on our sector of the front because the German Jastas were concentrated further south where Marshal Foch launched his great counter-offensive in front of Amiens on 8th August.

On that same day King George V arrived at Izel-le-Hameau to inspect all the squadrons there. The Camels of No 203 Squadron were lined up in front of the hangars, each Flight Commander standing at attention in front of his aeroplane. The King walked down the line with Brigadier General Pitcher, our Brigade Commander; immediately behind them were General Sir Henry Horne, Commander of the British First Army, with our CO, Major Raymond Collishaw, and the remainder of the entourage following them. The King stopped in front of me, said a few words, cracked a joke, at which we both smiled, and then continued on. Later, having completed the inspection he left with Sir Henry Horne in a staff-car to the cheers of all our squadron personnel who lined the road along which he passed. Peter, our brindle bulldog, gave his own special farewell by chasing after the car and barking loudly all the time.

It was later in the day that a special and urgent request came over the telephone from our Wing headquarters. They wanted the names of four pilots to be transferred to 201 Squadron at Bertangles. 201 had been making low-flying attacks all day in the fierce battle raging in front of Amiens and they had lost many pilots. Collishaw was away at the time so we three Flight Commanders gave the Wing details of four pilots who had recently joined our squadron. This did not suit the Wing Colonel who wanted four pilots with combat experience, so he picked the names himself, and telephoned his orders for Lieutenants Stone, Sehl, Carter and Sykes to be sent at once to 201 Squadron. They left with all their kit by lorry soon after midnight, sleeping in the lorry until their arrival at Bertangles.

Dick Stone, or Stoney as we always called him, had been in my flight since early summer and was due to go on leave. On 9th August at five o'clock in the afternoon he went on a low patrol with his new Flight Commander, Captain Kinkead, and was shot down and killed, on the German side of the lines, by a Fokker D.VII which dived on him out of low cloud. He was only 19 years of age and a member of a well-known legal family. I liked him immensely and felt very sad when I learned of his death.

Collishaw, who had already been awarded the DSO, DSC and DFC, now received notice of the award of a bar to his DSO. On 9th August, while out on a lone flight, he shot down a DFW which crashed near Hinges and on the following day he sent down two Fokkers, one seen to crash and the other out of control near Bray.

While out with my flight on an OP during the evening of August 11th, I shot down a D.VII out of control near Bray. On this same patrol, Sidebottom and Hales each shot down EA of a similar type out of control. Jack Hales was a Canadian who had recently joined my flight.

On 14th August the squadron moved to Allonville. Our new aerodrome was surrounded on three sides by a horseshoe-shaped wood which I had long used as a landmark when returning from patrols. We were entirely under canvas. The hangars were of a small portable type, our mess was a large marquee and we slept in bell-tents. On the opposite side of the aerodrome, bordering the wood, No 80 Squadron occupied permanent hangars and hutted living-quarters. They were commanded by Major Victor Bell, an Australian and the brother of B.C. Bell, a former Flight Commander in 3 Naval Squadron early in 1917 and later the CO of 10 Naval.

On the following day while out with my flight on an early morning OP, fog began to roll up, the weather closed in and we became separated. I decided to land in a field at Franvillers to wait until it cleared. Having telephoned Collishaw to report where I was, a couple of mechanics later arrived to start up the engine of my Camel and I landed back at Allonville about 10 o'clock. Later in the afternoon, Collishaw went out alone and shot down an EA and at six o'clock in the evening I led the whole squadron, escorting DH4s of 205 Squadron on a bombing raid to Péronne. We had a trouble-free trip and all the Camels and DH4s returned home safely.

These escort patrols were quite different operations from the OPs already mentioned. Our freedom of action was much restricted, obliged as we were to remain within close range of the formation under escort.

Normally we escorted two-seat bomber or photograph-reconnaissance formations which we met over a rendezvous point behind our lines where we formated on them, close behind, before setting course for the target.

This type of formation made it very difficult for EA to get past the escorting fighters from astern and any that did were assured of a hot reception from the rear machine-guns of the two-seaters. Attacks made by the enemy on either flank of the formation were baulked by the outside members of the escort whose efforts were augmented, when necessary, by the gunners of the escorted force.

The most vulnerable positions were the rearmost members of the escort but the tighter they maintained their formation the safer they were as EA usually disliked tackling those which were well closed-up.

When a whole squadron carried out an escort one flight kept close formation on the bomber/reconnaissance machines and the other two flew stepped up and positioned to prevent any high attacks which the enemy might develop at some distance from the main formation.

At 10.30 on the following morning we again escorted No 205 Squadron to Péronne and on our way home a flight of Fokker D.VIII monoplanes dived on us from above and behind but did not press home the attack. This was the first occasion on which we had seen the new Fokker monoplane fighter and, I believe, it was the first time it had been reported on the Western Front. It was probably the first batch which were sent to the front at the beginning of August. In some aspects it was similar in appearance to a Fokker D.VII with the bottom plane removed and equipped with a rotary engine. On landing back at Allonville I found that Sergeant-Pilot Fletcher, who had recently joined 'B' Flight, was missing and I understand he was later reported shot down and killed. All the DH4s returned safely to their aerodrome at Bois de Roche.

During the afternoon the commander of our Fifth Brigade, Brigadier General L.E.O. Charlton, visited us to get information about the new Fokker in which he showed great interest as I gave him a description of its appearance.

After lunch on 17th August I flew over to Bois de Roche to meet Monty Wright who was an observer in 205 Squadron. We discussed the two bombing raids on Péronne and reminisced about our schooldays. At his invitation I spent the night at Bois de Roche.

Some time after this I was badly stricken with enteritis and was sent to an army hospital at Pont Remy where I remained for about ten days. I felt pretty awful for the best part of a week but the two nurses who looked after me were very kind and sympathetic. A fellow-patient in the same ward was Major Goble, the Commanding Officer of No 205 Squadron. In charge of the ward was Sister Jackman, a very kind soul but with little sense of humour and easily upset. One of the Ward Orderlies, named Moore, knowing this often pulled her leg, and as a result she would frequently lose her temper. This, of course, only encouraged him to tease her even more.

I returned to our squadron at Allonville shortly before the end of August. From the beginning of the Amiens Offensive it had been mainly a month of low-flying missions combined with OPs and some escorts. The enemy was attacked constantly by our low-level bombing and intense machine-gun fire. As the Fifth Brigade summary for 29th August states:

> Patrols of No 203 Squadron dropped 20 bombs on a convoy of lorries on the Péronne-Rancourt road and fired 2500 rounds into objectives in this vicinity. Also, 20 bombs were dropped on Grand Prix road east of the Somme and 2,500 rounds fired. Captain Whealy's patrol dropped 20 bombs on parties of men in the vicinity of Bussu east of Péronne. The bombs were seen to explode among these troops. 2,800 rounds were fired into about 200 lorries on different main roads east of Péronne. Eight bombs were dropped on enemy huts and transport at Aizecourt, causing a large fire. 600 rounds were fired from a low altitude. 25 bombs were dropped onto a battalion of infantry. The bombs were seen to fall among the troops who disappeared into shrubbery and were dispersed. About 100 lorries were also attacked, 3,200 rounds being fired at them. 32 bombs were dropped and 4,400 rounds fired at various ground targets.

Two of our pilots were posted to Home Establishment during August, 'Kiwi' Beamish who had been with the squadron since its formation in 1916, was now Flight Commander of 'A' Flight, had shot down many EA and held the DSC and Louis Bawlf who had also served with us for more than a year.

I was very saddened to hear, on arriving back at Allonville, that Jack Hales had been killed on 23rd August when his elevator controls had been severed by Archie and he crashed. We had flown together in 'B' Flight and shared a bell-tent at Allonville. He had been very kind to me during the night I was stricken with enteritis. The day I arrived back in the squadron, Collishaw and I went by car to try to find Jack's crashed Camel which fell in the vicinity of Bray. During our search I was directed to a dugout where I was told I might get the required information. An officer came up the steps to meet me and who should it be but my cousin, Charles Rochford, whom I had not seen since early in the war. Charlie was in charge of the burial of the British and German dead left on the battlefield. I introduced him to Collishaw and we all had a round of drinks. Unfortunately he could not give us any information about the crashed Camel.

He joined us in the car and we set off in search of the wreck. On the way we saw hundreds of dead British and German soldiers and horses lying just where they had fallen. It was a gruesome sight and the stench was terrible. Our search for Hales' Camel was in vain. We had Peter, our bulldog, with us and having said farewell to Charlie were about to return to Allonville when Peter got involved in a fight with a black Labrador retriever. Peter grabbed a front leg of the Labrador which promptly grabbed Peter's ear. Eventually we pulled them apart, but Peter's ear was torn through and needed attention when we got back. Unfortunately the wound turned septic and took rather a long time to heal up.

On 27th August while out on an OP, Whealy and Britnell each shot down a DFW two-seater, both of these crashing near Combles. I took 'B' Flight out in the morning and afternoon of 31st August on special low-level bombing and reconnaissance missions, attacking various enemy targets and gaining as much information as possible as to the German line of retreat.

CHAPTER XII

FINALE AND FOLDED WINGS

On 3rd September Yvone Kirkpatrick returned to the squadron and my flight, having fully recovered from the wound he received when we were bombed on the night of 31st July.

Our first victory of the month was scored by Art Whealy. When leading his flight on an OP, he shot down a Fokker D.VII which crashed in Havrincourt Wood. On the same day, 4th September, I took my flight out at 5.30 a.m. to bomb enemy troops before carrying out an OP.

The following day Collishaw, when flying alone, saw a Fokker D.VII attacking one of our balloons and shot it down in flames on our side of the lines near Inchy en Artois. That afternoon I had my flight on an OP and after we had been patrolling for about an hour a piston of my engine seized-up and I was forced to land in a field at Hébécourt, close to an Australian Army camp. The Major in command of the unit came out to meet me and we went to his office where I rang up the squadron, gave details of the mishap and arranged for spare parts to be brought out to the machine.

Late in the afternoon Rogers, my fitter, and another mechanic arrived and at once set about removing the faulty cylinder and broken piston. Eventually the new parts were fitted and I climbed into the cockpit and started up the engine. I ran it slowly at first and gradually increased the revs to the maximum. The engine ran smoothly and everything seemed to be in order so I decided to take off for Allonville. The field was not very large and there were shell craters here and there which I had to avoid. I had Rogers and the other mechanic hang on to my wing-tips to hold back the machine then I opened up the throttle to its full extent, waved them away and shot into the air after a very short run.

I realised as I flew into the setting sun that it would be nearly dark when I landed at Allonville. However, I was fated never to arrive there, for I had been flying only a few minutes and was at a mere 1,000 feet, when the engine backfired, vibrated violently and completely seized-up. I closed the throttle, turned off the petrol, switched off and nosed the Camel downwards to maintain flying speed. Beneath me was an area of trenches and shell craters – part of the old Somme battlefield. Turning into wind I finally made a 'pancake' landing across a trench. The undercarriage collapsed and the nose of the machine hit the parapet of the trench, pushing back the engine so that the air intakes were close up against my knees. Although the machine was completely wrecked, I was uninjured and, unfastening my belt, was able to climb out of the cockpit.

It was almost dark as I saw the lights of an army lorry travelling along a nearby road. I hurried over there and stopped it. The driver informed me that I was near Chuignolles and gave me a lift to his unit. I saw the Commanding Officer and, after telephoning Collishaw to say where I had crashed, went to the Officers' Mess and had a drink with him. Later, some of the officers took me to a hut where I was able to rest on a bed while they played a game of poker. I did not have long to sleep for in the early hours of the morning Warrant Officer Finch arrived to take me back to Allonville. He said he had seen the crashed Camel which was a write-off and that they would collect it later.

On arrival at Allonville, soon after dawn, I was told we were to move back to Izel-le-Hameau at once. There was no time for more sleep so, after a good breakfast, I took off with my flight and landed at Izel-le-Hameau at about 10.30. Before leaving Allonville, Collishaw had also informed me that he had received news from No 70 Squadron that my brother Bill was missing. So, in the afternoon, I flew over to them to get some further details. I was told that Bill's Flight Commander, Captain Forman, had led the squadron on an OP and, when they were a long distance over the enemy lines, were attacked by a much superior force of Fokkers and a dog-fight had developed. The Clerget-engined Camels suffered heavy losses and Forman and my brother were missing, and later it was reported that both had been taken prisoner. When Bill returned home after the Armistice he explained that during the fight his engine had been hit and put out of action and he was forced to land in a field. He was first taken to a local prison where he met Forman. From there they managed to escape during the night and were at large for a few days but were eventually recaptured and were then taken to a POW camp at Rastatt.

On our return to Izel-le-Hameau we did not go into our old quarters in the orchard as they were now occupied by No 209 Squadron commanded by Major Teddy Gerrard DSC. We were under canvas and our Camels were housed in small portable canvas hangars. However, we did have a wooden hut as a mess.

At 7 o'clock on the morning of 7th September our whole squadron went up on an OP, mine being the leading and bottom flight. Five Fokkers were observed and attacked and I shot one down which crashed near Bourlon Wood. This was Kirkpatrick's first patrol since returning to 'B' Flight.

During the week we were notified that I had been awarded the Distinguished Flying Cross so, about the middle of the month I went home on leave during which I attended Buckingham Palace to receive, from King George V, this DFC which had so recently been awarded to me. The investiture took place in the courtyard of the Palace and the King was accompanied by Prince Albert, later to become King George VI.

During my absence Sidebottom took over command of 'B' Flight. In the afternoon of 20th September the whole squadron went out on an OP and got into a dog-fight with 14 Fokkers. 'B' Flight were flying at about 17,000 feet when Sidebottom made a sharp turn and dived. As he did so, some of the EA attacked. One made for Kirkpatrick and he got separated from the flight when evading it.

Coghill had three Fokkers after him and as one of these shot past him he got on its tail and fired a short burst whereupon one of its wings crumpled up and it fell near Haynecourt. The other two continued to attack Coghill but he managed to evade them, though some of their bullets made holes in his wings.

Meanwhile 'A' and 'C' Flights were also involved in this fight and Breakey, Britnell and Skinner each got a D.VII down out of control. Cruise, too, was seen to shoot down in flames a Fokker, the pilot of which jumped out with a parachute. This was one of the first attempts to descend from an aeroplane by parachute to be seen on the Western Front. Unfortunately the parachute failed to open properly in this case and the German pilot was killed. Our troops wrapped him in his parachute and buried him where he fell. Cruise and Milne failed to return from this patrol and the former was later reported to have been shot down and killed.

When it was learned later at Brigade HQ that the German pilot had been buried in his parachute, Collishaw received orders to recover it. A party was sent out to open the grave, retrieve the parachute and then rebury the pilot. The parachute was brought back to Izel-le-Hameau where it was hung up on a tree in the orchard for at least a week in order to clear the stench from it which was horrible.

Air activity was mounting up during the latter part of September and on the 24th Sidebottom and Coghill each shot down an EA. While I was still on leave a combined attack by 14 Camels of our squadron and 11 SE5as of No 40 Squadron was made on the German aerodrome at Lieu St Amand, escorted by Bristol Fighters of No 22 Squadron. After 40 Squadron had attacked first, dropping bombs on the hangars, one of which caught on fire and obtaining several direct hits on huts, 203 Squadron, led by Collishaw, then went in, setting three hangars on fire and obtaining two direct hits on a fourth. Two large huts were also seen burning. The living quarters were attacked with machine-gun fire and smoke was seen to come from one building. A DFW two-seater on the ground was shot up and burst into flames and Woodhouse attacked fifty cavalry on a road, causing heavy casualties. In all, 88 bombs were dropped on this raid and Fokkers were shot down by Collishaw, Breakey, Britnell and Coghill. The following extract from a letter by Kirkpatrick to his parents gives a vivid account of his part in this raid:

I told you that from 12 noon to 2 p.m. today would be pretty exciting, but I had no idea I would have experienced so much excitement and yet be able to write to tell you about it. I cannot tell you what the job was, but this is partly what happened.

We broke up formation and dived on our objective. I dropped my bombs on something which I thought would appreciate them and then at a height of 100 feet charged about firing my guns at things on the ground till they would not fire any more. Then I decided to come home. The Archie was awful and also the machine-gun fire from the ground. I was trying to climb up and join some of our machines flying westwards, when suddenly my engine stopped. I picked a field and was just going to land when I thought I would switch over to my gravity tank. The engine restarted and I decided to try to get home. I was about eleven miles east of the lines and none of our other machines was in sight, so I decided to hedge-hop near to the ground to avoid Archie.

My engine wasn't going very well and the west wind was against me. You should have seen the expression of people's faces. I flew over a sunken road and saw two fat old Huns walking calmly along with their hands in their pockets; they simply stared at me with mouths wide open. Then I saw two Fokkers diving on me. I simply tore round trees and church steeples with them firing at me. After what seemed like years, I saw some trees, which I thought I knew were on our side of the lines. The machine-gun fire got very fierce, then suddenly stopped. I looked over the side of the cockpit and saw some Scotsmen waving to me. Some relief, believe me.

While I was hedge-hopping I saw one of our machines land under control on the Hun side of the lines and on arriving home I found we had three pilots missing. A bullet had gone through my tank and the petrol was pouring out.

On the following day low-bombing attacks were carried out in conjunction with operations by the Canadian Corps. Troops and transport were heavily bombed and machine-gunned on the bridges crossing the Sensée Canal and the Canal de L'Escaut. Direct hits and casualties were observed.

I returned from leave at the end of September and learned that, a day or so before, Breakey had destroyed an LVG two-seater and Sidebottom a Fokker while out on Special Missions.

On October 1st I led 'B' Flight on three Special Missions bombing and machine-gunning troops and other targets near Cambrai. On one of these trips Sidebottom shot down a Fokker which crashed near Naves.

The following day 'B' Flight carried out two OPs during which we also attacked enemy balloons one of which we drove down damaged at Hordain and Sidebottom shot down out of control another Fokker. Britnell, when out with 'C' Flight, got a balloon down in flames and Breakey, leading 'A' Flight, sent down a Fokker which crashed near Morenchies and Skinner shot down a second of the type. During this week it was announced that Whealy had been awarded the DFC.

On 9th October in the afternoon I took 'B' Flight on an OP during which Sidebottom and I attacked and shot down in flames a Rumpler two-seater which crashed near St Aubert.

About the middle of October an example occurred of the excessive high spirits which from time to time broke out in our squadrons.

Unfortunately, in this particular case it ended in tragedy. On the evening in question one of the squadrons at Izel-leHameau were having a party when some of its members decided to raid the mess of another squadron. Armed with Very light pistols one or two climbed on to the roof and fired them down the chimney. This started off a 'battle' between the two squadrons and very soon Very lights were being fired into the air in all directions, some of them landing on roofs of the hangars. Some of the more sober fellows on the aerodrome climbed up and kicked these off before they could start a fire. It was like a gigantic Guy Fawkes Night celebration and those concerned seemed to be enjoying it a lot until someone firing a Very pistol at random, hit the CO of another squadron behind an ear, severely injuring him. He was taken to hospital where he died during the night. It was a tragic ending to a very wild evening.

Before the end of the month Collishaw received orders to report to the Air Ministry in London and handed over the squadron to Major T.F. Hazell DSO MC DFC, its first Commanding Officer who was not a Canadian.

My CO and old friend, Raymond Collishaw, left 203 Squadron on 22nd October. I travelled with him in the squadron car to the aerodrome at Marquise and we took with us Peter, the squadron's bulldog, as Collie was hoping to take Peter to England with him. But the regulations did not allow this and he had to return to the squadron with me after I had said farewell to Collie and wished him good luck.

During the time he was on the Western Front, Collie had shot down about 60 enemy aircraft most of them when he was a Flight Commander in 10 Naval Squadron, and the final 20 between June and October 1918, when in command of 203 Squadron. He was now promoted to Lieutenant Colonel and when he reported to the Air Ministry was informed of his posting back to Canada to become Senior Staff Officer to Brigadier General C.G. Hoare, who was in charge of the entire Canadian pilot training scheme. Early in 1919, however, he was offered a permanent commission in the RAF which he accepted. After a long and successful career in the RAF he retired in 1943 as an Air Vice-Marshal.

Another stalwart who left us a month earlier was Art Whealy. One of the Canadian pilots who joined No 3 (Naval) Squadron at Vert Galant in February 1917, he left it for 9 Naval in May 1917, and returned when we went to Walmer in November 1917. His total of air victories was about 27 and he had only recently been awarded the DFC to add to his DSC and bar. As the highly competent Flight Commander of 'C' Flight he was popular with us all in 203 Squadron.

Hazell had only been in command of the squadron a couple of days when it moved to an aerodrome occupied until recently by a German squadron. This was Bruille, a small French village, and it was here for the first time, that we were billetted on the local French people. Our mess was in the main street and outside it, parked off the road, was the CO's sleeping-quarters. This was a nicely furnished hut which Collishaw, when based at Izel-le-Hameau, had fixed on a trailer ready to be attached to a lorry and towed to our new destination whenever we moved aerodromes.

On both 26th and 27th October I carried out low OPs with my flight. During the former I attacked an armoured Hannover but my burst of fire at close-range had little or no effect as the EA dived away. During an OP on 27th we encountered an armoured AEG near St Saulve which I attacked at close-range, again with indecisive result.

The final day of this month brought success for, while out with my flight on a high OP, we encountered a large formation of Fokkers. I dived on one of them, opened fire at close-range and he fell out of control.

Shortly after assuming command Hazell, who I suspect, had been looking at squadron personnel records, commented on the rather long time I had been with them and suggested I might like a spell on Home Establishment. This was the last thing I wanted as not only were our tails well up and victory in sight but I was enjoying my flying as much as ever. When I explained this to him Hazell said, 'All right, Tich, but just let me know whenever you feel you've have enough.'

At the beginning of November we learned that the DFC had been awarded to H.W. Skinner. He was no longer with our squadron, having been badly wounded in the arm and taken to hospital after making a crash-landing behind the British lines. Collishaw had taken him and Fricker out and they were straffing a German balloon when he had been attacked by a Fokker. Skinner was among the last of the RNAS pilots to join our squadron when it was still 3 Naval and had shot down and crashed four EA, the final one being a Fokker which he got on 2nd October, the day on which he was wounded.

The German retreat continued at ever-increasing speed and every day we went out on offensive patrols during which we met some large formations of Fokkers. They were very cautious, showed little offensive spirit and tried to lure us well over to their own side of the lines. We tried to get into position to attack, but never seemed able to come to grips with them.

On 4th November our whole squadron went up in the afternoon with orders to clear the sky of EA. At 10,000 feet we saw four Fokkers away to the east and went after them. 'A' and 'C' Flights were flying above 'B' Flight which I was leading. As 'B' Flight approached near to these Fokkers, hoping to attack them, they dived away from us. We went after them but they outpaced us and we were unable to get within shooting range.

A few days later, at the end of an OP, we flew low over Mons from which town the Germans had now retreated more than four years after the famous British retreat from the same town. Flags were flying from every house and the people in the streets waved to us with great enthusiasm as we skimmed over the housetops.

It was now rumoured that an armistice was expected to be declared at 11 o'clock on the morning of 11th November. At 7.15 that morning I led 'B' Flight on a high OP. We patrolled for 1¼ hours but saw no EA in the sky. As soon as we landed we received the official news that an armistice was to be signed at 11 o'clock.

To the personnel of 203 Squadron this came as something of an anti-climax and there was none of the emotion and hysteria which took place among civilians in France and England. Some of us went that evening to a variety performance given by the First Army concert party which was known as the 'Rouge et Noirs' and was probably the best organization of its type on the Western Front.

All real purpose in our flying now seemed to have come to an end and for me, at any rate, the day-to-day life in the squadron became somewhat boring. When the weather was suitable, we carried out Balloon-Line Patrols and sometimes formation practice.

One day, when it was very foggy, some of us went to Lille with Hazell in the squadron car. It was my first and only visit to this large French city though I had often seen it from the air when flying on patrols. We arrived in Lille about noon and had an excellent lunch in the Officers' Club which occupied one of the large hotels. Afterwards we walked around the town amusing ourselves in one way or another. There seemed to be plenty of food in the shops and all sorts of wonderful jewellery. The patisseries were well stocked with pastries, cakes and all kinds of sweets. Prices were, of course, much higher than before the war – probably about four times as high. After having tea we returned to Bruille.

We moved from Bruille to Auberchicourt on 24th November and were again billetted in the nearby village. McKay, who had not long been with us, and I found a billet in the home of Monsieur and Madame Martin, charming people with two delightful daughters –Jeanne and Mimi. Monsieur Martin was the owner of a sugar factory situated next door to his house. Jeanne, unlike Mimi, spoke English very well, and was also quite an artist. She was also very intelligent and her conversation was always interesting. At the same time she was very outspoken and when I asked her to draw a pencil portrait of me she at first replied quite bluntly that she was not interested in doing so. Nevertheless, she later drew one, without being asked again and presented it to me. Unfortunately I lost this in World War Two when most of my household goods were destroyed by a German bomb when in store. Jeanne hated bad manners and told us that most of the German officers showed courtesy towards women during their occupation of the area.

We set up our Officers' Mess in an empty *estaminet* in the main street of Auberchicourt and many French civilians, returning to their homes after the Armistice, seemed to think it was still an *estaminet* so we had all sorts of strange people call in requesting food and drink.

One evening when we were having dinner a Belgian soldier in uniform came in. He told Kirkpatrick that he wanted '*un grand morceau*'. Bingo Bingham, the Mess Secretary, got him a good meal with plenty of drink to quench his thirst. The result was that after dinner he was 'revving' in great style and an impromptu party soon started up in the mess. Bingo, wearing a top hat, kept filling the Belgian's pockets with biscuits as he sang songs and demonstrated Belgian dances. A few more drinks, some very mixed, and he collapsed suddenly and broke into tears when he realised that he ought to be in Douai that night to be reunited with his family. The tears poured down his face and he was in a state of despair. He tried to walk away down the road but soon fell over. So we carried him back into the mess and settled him down on the sofa where he soon fell asleep. The next morning one of our transport drivers took him partly on his way in the tender and we never saw him again.

On 8th December I flew my Camel, E4386, for the last time, landing first at Saultain where I had lunch with No 209 Squadron. Afterwards I visited No 210 Squadron before returning to Auberchicourt.

On the morning of 9th December as I bade farewell to Monsieur and Madame Martin and their daughters. Madame's parting words to me were: '*Mimi a beaucoup de chagrin parce que le Capitaine s'en va*'. And so I left Auberchicourt for Boulogne and England on leave. It was sad to leave all my friends especially as by then I had been with 203 Squadron for nearly two years and was the only remaining original pilot member who had served with it since its period of formation at Dunkirk. In that time I had accumulated a total of 755 operational hours in the air and of these 742 had been flown on the Western Front.

Before leaving France I closed my Log Book with the following remarks:

Left No 203 Squadron on the 9th December 1918 after being with them since 24th January 1917. I shall always remember those two years as among the happiest of my life. At all times we were all a happy family and stuck together through thick and thin.

EPILOGUE

I remained on leave until the end of December when I was posted to Weston-on-the-Green near Oxford, where the Commanding Officer was Major R.B. Munday who had been my instructor on the Curtiss JN4 at Cranwell in 1916. Life was pretty boring here though we did manage to get into Oxford in the evening fairly often and one very enjoyable dance took place in the Officers' Mess.

I did very little flying — I think only two flights in a Camel and one in a Sopwith Snipe. This last was my one and only flight in a Snipe and I found it quite a nice aeroplane to handle. With its 220 hp BR2 rotary-engine it was slightly speedier and better in climb than the Camel but it had not the wonderful manoeuvrability of the latter.

None of these flights was entered in my Log Book.

Early in April I left the RAF to return to civilian life. Little did I realise then that 21 years later I was to rejoin the RAF as a Flight Lieutenant in the RAFVR during World War Two. After two years of administrative duties in Balloon Command, I returned to flying in 1941, taking a refresher course on Tiger Moths and Miles Magisters at Marshall's aerodrome at Cambridge. I was then posted to the Flying Wing of No 2 Radio School, Yatesbury where I was in charge of two Proctor Flights whose pilots were mainly Poles and Czechs.

From Yatesbury I was posted to RAF Halton in December 1943 to take charge of the Station Flight and there I remained until my return to civilian life in June 1945.

In conclusion I am proud to say that my three sons maintained the tradition of service by sea and air in the war years of 1939-1945.

The eldest, James, was in the RNVR and for a considerable time was engaged on convoy escort operations in both the Atlantic and Mediterranean.

Edmund was a member of an RAF Liberator crew operating in the Far East. He received an immediate award of the Distinguished Flying Medal.

David, the youngest, was a pilot in the Fleet Air Arm.

APPENDIX 1
No 3 (Naval) Squadron / No 203 Squadron RAF

No 203 Squadron RAF can probably claim to be the oldest squadron in the RAF. It was first formed as a Naval Unit at Eastchurch under the command of Lieutenant C.R. Samson in November 1911. In August 1914 Samson took the unit to Ostend with a varied collection of aeroplanes and armoured vehicles. It roved around in Belgium and Northern France attacking Germans wherever it found them until it was ordered to move to Tenedos to take part in the Gallipoli campaign. Later it moved to Imbros and it was there that Squadron Commander R. Bell Davies won the Victoria Cross. At the end of the Dardanelles expedition the squadron returned to England and was disbanded.

In December 1916 it was re-formed as No 3 (Naval) Squadron at No 1 Wing RNAS, Dunkirk. It moved from Dunkirk to Vert Galant on 10th February 1917, under the command of Squadron Commander R.H. Mulock DSO to be attached to the RFC and was equipped with single-seater Sopwith Pups. Movements of the squadron are given below:

Dunkirk to Vert Galant	10th February 1917	attached RFC
Vert Galant to Bertangles	28th February 1917	attached RFC
Bertangles to Marieux	26th March 1917	attached RFC
Marieux to Furnes	15th June 1917	RNAS

Early in July 1917 the squadron was re-equipped with Sopwith Camels powered by BR1 rotary engines

Furnes to Bray Dunes	5th September 1917	RNAS
Bray Dunes to Walmer	1st November 1917	RNAS

Walmer to Bray Dunes	2nd January 1918	RNAS
Bray Dunes to Mont St Eloi	1st March 1918	RFC
Mont St Eloi to Treizennes	28th March 1918	RFC

On 1st April 1918 the unit became No 203 Squadron RAF

Treizennes to Estrée Blanche	9th April 1918	RAF
Estrée Blanche to Izel-le-Hameau	15th May 1918	RAF
Izel-le-Hameau to Allonville	14th August 1918	RAF
Allonville to Izel-le-Hameau	6th September 1918	RAF
Izel-le-Hameau to Bruille	24th October 1918	RAF
Bruille to Auberchicourt	24th November 1918	RAF
Auberchicourt to Tournai	22nd December 1918	RAF

Wings served under:
22nd Wing, RFC
13th Wing, RFC
No 4 Wing, RNAS
10th Wing, RFC and RAF

Brigades served under:
1st Brigade RAF
5th Brigade RFC and RAF

APPENDIX 2

No 3 (Naval) Squadron / No 203 Squadron RAF

Summary of EA shot down 1917–18

1917	*Month*		*EA shot down*
	February		2
	March		13
	April		45
	May		15
	June		1
	July		10
	August		3
	September		19
		Total	108

1918			
	January		6
	February		4
	March		38
	April		12
	May		50
	June		14
	July		22
	August		12
	September		18
	October		7
		Total	183

While the squadron was attached to RFC and RAF Offensive Patrols, Line Patrols and Escorts were carried out and also bombing and shooting-up ground targets. When on the coast with the RNAS, Escorts to the Fleet operating off Ostend and Zeebrugge were its function. Also, Gothas attacking England were engaged and Offensive Sweeps from the coast to Ypres and Escorts to RNAS bombers and photo-reconnaissance aeroplanes were flown.

APPENDIX 3

Captain L.H. Rochford, DSC and bar, DFC
No 3 Squadron RNAS and No 203 Squadron RAF
March 1917–October 1918

*Record of combats against enemy aircraft with, at right,
the author's contemporary assessments of results.*

1917

Date	Serial	Type	Mission	Location	Enemy	Result
March 4	N5199	Pup	Escort	Manancourt	Albatros	Decisive
April 22	N6207	"	Escort	Cambrai	Albatros	Indecisive
May 1	N6207	"	Escort	Epinoy	Albatros Sct	Indecisive
May 20	N6461	"	OP	NE. Bullecourt	Albatros Sct	Decisive
May 28	Betty II	"	OP	SE. Arras	Albatros 2 Str	Indecisive
May 30	N6461	"	OP	Bullecourt	Albatros Sct	Indecisive
July 7	N6162	"	HA patrol	Ostend	Seaplane	Decisive
Sept 5	B3807	Camel	OP	Leke	Albatros Sct	Decisive
Sept 11	B3798	"	O Sweep	Thorout	Albatros Sct	Decisive
Sept 12	B3798	"	O Sweep	Westende	Albatros Sct	Indecisive
Sept 23	B3807	"	HAAP	Middelkerke	DFW 2 Str	Indecisive
Oct 1	B3798	"	FPP	Westende	DFW 2 Str	Indecisive
Oct 20	B3807	"	OP	Dixmude	Albatros Sct	Indecisive
Oct 22	B3807	"	HAAP	Middelkerke	DFW 2 Str	Indecisive
Oct 27	B3798	"	OP	Westende/Slype	DFW 2 Str	Indecisive

1918

Date	Aircraft		Mission	Location	Enemy aircraft	Result
Jan 22	B6401		Gun test	Nieuport	DFW 2 Str	Indecisive
Jan 28	B6401	"	O Sweep	Roulers	DFW 2 Str	Indecisive
Jan 28	B6401	"	O Sweep	Houthulst	DFW 2 Str	Decisive
Jan 30	B6401	"	HOP	Gheluvelt	Albatros Scts 2	Decisive
Feb 2	B6401	"	HA patrol	Middelkerke	LVG 2 Str	Indecisive
Feb 17	B6401	"	Escort	Houthulst	Albatros 2 Str	Indecisive
Feb 21	B6401	"	HOP	Gheluvelt	Albatros Sct	Indecisive
March 10	B7203	"	OP	S of Douai	Albatros 2 Str	Indecisive
March 10	B7203	"	OP	Nr. Lens	Albatros Scts	3 indecisive
March 12	B7203	"	OP	Brebières	Albatros 2 Str	Decisive
March 12	B7203	"	OP	Bois de l'Ecluse	Albatros 2 Str	Indecisive
March 16	B7203	"	OP	Gavrelle	Hannover 2 Str	Decisive
March 18	B7222	"	OP	Haubourdin	Rumpler 2 Str	Indecisive
March 21	B7222	"	OP	Douai	Albatros Sct / Albatros Scts	Decisive / 2 indecisive
March 21	B7203	"	OP	Vaulx	Albatros 2 Str / A wreck	Decisive with flight

Date		Serial	Flight	Location	Enemy aircraft	Result
March 22	"	B7203	OP	Boursies / Marquion	Albatros Sct / Albatros Sct	Decisive / Indecisive
March 23	"	B7203	OP	Bauvin	DFW 2 Str	Indecisive
March 23	"	B7203	W/T patrol	Armentières	Rumpler 2 Str	Indecisive
March 24	"	B7203	OP	Beaumetz	Albatros Scts / Pfalz Scts	Decisive / 2 indecisive
April 22	"	B7197	O Sweep	Merville	Albatros Sct	2 indecisive
May 3	"	B7197	O Sweep	Pont du Hem	LVG 2 Str	Indecisive
May 9	"	B7197	Test flight	Pacaut Wood	DFW 2 Str	Indecisive
May 9	"	B7197	Reece escort	E. Pacaut Wood	DFW 2 Str	Indecisive
May 15	"	D3353	OP	N. Estaires	DFW 2 Str	Decisive
May 17	"	B7197	O Sweep	N. Estaires	Pfalz Scts	Decisive / Decisive with flight / Several indecisive
May 19	"	D3371	HOP	Nr. Merville	DFW 2 Str / LVG 2 Str	Decisive / Indecisive
May 21	"	D3413	OP	Neuf Berquin	DFW 2 Str	Decisive
May 27	"	D3413	Special Mission	N. Morville	Rumpler 2 Str	Indecisive
May 28	"	D3413	OP	Neuve Eglise	Pfalz Scts	Indecisive
May 31	"	D3417	OP	Carvin	DFW 2 Str	Indecisive

Date	Serial		Mission	Location	Aircraft	Result
June 1	D3403	"	Special Mission	Festubert	DFW 2 Str	Indecisive
June 5	D3417	"	Special Mission	La Bassée	LVG 2 Str	Decisive
June 7	D3417	"	OP	Neuve Eglise / Nr. La Bassée	Fokker Dr 1 / Fokker Dr 1	Decisive / Indecisive
July 20	D9618	"	OP	Lestrem	DFW 2 Str	Decisive
July 22	D9618	"	Special Mission	Dorignies	Aerodrome Strafe	Bombs & shoot-up
July 22	D9585	"	OP	Carvin / Festubert	Fokker D. 7 / Fokker D. 7	Decisive / Decisive
July 25	D9618	"	OP	La Bassée	Fokker D. 7	Decisive
July 28	D9618	"	OP	Vitry	DFW 2 Strs	Indecisive
Aug 11	D9618	"	OP	E of Bray	Fokker D. 7	Decisive
Sept 7	C197	"	OP	Bois de Bourlon	Fokker D. 7	Decisive
Oct 9	E4386	"	OP	St. Aubert	Rumpler 2 Str	Decisive
Oct 26	D3230	"	OP (low)	Aulnoy	Hannover 2 Str	Indecisive
Oct 27	D4386	"	OP (low)	St. Saulve	A.E.G	Indecisive
Oct 29	D4386	"	OP	E of Bray	Fokker D.7	Decisive

KEY:
OP — Offensive Patrol; HA — Hostile Aircraft Patrol; HAAP — Hostile Artillery Aircraft Patrol; HOP — High Offensive Patrol; FPP — Fleet Protection Patrol.

APPENDIX 4

Officers who served at some time in No 3 (Naval) Squadron / No 203 Squadron RAF between 1st February 1917 and 11th November 1918

Serial Numbers of the aircraft involved are in parentheses.

Abbott, R.F.P. *Wounded, 17th August 1917*
Adam, O.P. *Killed in action, 1st April 1918. (B3798)*
Adams, E.F.
Airey, H.P.
Allen, Hugh *Killed in action, 6th July 1917*
Allison, J.L. *Missing, 18th March 1918. (B7217)*
Amos, J.W.P. *Injured accidentally, 27th August 1917*
Anderson, G.B.
Armstrong, F.C., DSC *Killed in action, 25th March 1918. (B7218)*
Archer, A.W. *Wounded, 20th October 1917*
Bawlf, D.L. *Killed accidentally, 21st April 1918. (B3795)*
Barbour, D.B.
Beamish, H.F., DSC
Bell, B.C., DSO, DSC
Bennett, S.L. *Killed in action, 29th April 1917*
Benstead, F.E.C.
Berlyn, R.C. *Wounded in foot, 7th April 1918*
Bingham, P.W. (Recording Officer)
Black, F.G. *Wounded, 21st September 1918*
*Breadner, L.S., DSC
Broad, H.S. *Wounded, 11th May 1917*
Bricknell, F.J.S.
Brown, A. Roy, DSC
Brown, C.F.
Calder, P.B.

Campbell, K.D. *POW, 10th March 1918. (B7230)*

Carter, A.W., DSC

Carter, W.A.W.

Casey, F.D., DSC *Killed accidentally, 11th August 1917*

Chisam, W.H. *Wounded, 26th March 1918*

Coghill, W.H. POW, *26th September 1918*

*Collishaw, R., DSO, DSC, OBE, DFC

Cooper, J.S. (Sgt Pilot)

Coyle, P. (Rigging Officer)

Crane, J.W.

Cruise, M.G. *Killed in action 20th September 1918. (E4409)*

Daniells, J.D. POW, *11th May 1917*

Denison, John *Killed in action 13th April 1918. (D3347)*

Devereux, C.S.

Dixie, N.C. *Wounded, 22nd April, 1918*

Ellwood, A.B., DSC

England, B.H. (Stores Officer)

Fall, J.S.T. DSC

Fidgen, A.C. (Sgt Pilot)

Fletcher, P.M. (Sgt Pilot) *POW, 16th August 1918. (D9595)*

Fricker, A.J. *POW, 4th July 1918. (D3370)*

Garland, A.H.

George, F.A.

Gibbons, F.G.

Glen, J.A., DSC

Goodnow, W.W. (USA)

Graham, G.W.

Haig, D.A. (Armament Officer)

Hales, J.P. *Killed in action, 23rd August, 1918. (D9671)*

Hall, N.D. *Shot down and made POW, 3rd September 1917*

Harrower, G.S. *Wounded and sent to hospital, 23rd September 1917*

Hayne, E.T., DSC, DFC

*Hazell, T.F., DSO, MC, DFC

Horton, C.R.R. *Injured accidentally, 28th September 1918. (E4400)*

Hosken, S.T.

Hunter, J.W.

Ireland, H.M. DSC

Jones, W.G. (Sgt Pilot)

Kemp, F.H. (Stores Officer)

Kerby, H.S. DSC

Kirkpatrick, Y.E.S. *Wounded in bomb raid 31st July 1918. Returned to squadron, 3rd September 1918*

Le Boutillier, O.C.

Ledgood, F.A.

Lick, C.H. *Wounded in bomb raid, 31st July 1918. Returned later, 17th October 1918*

Lightbody, R.R. (Sgt Pilot) *Killed in action, 15th September 1918. (E4404)*

Lindsay, B.T. (Sgt Pilot)

Lindsay, L.L. *Landed in sea off Ostend, rescued and taken to hospital,in Dunkirk July 1917*

Little, R.A., DSO, DSC *Killed in action, 27th May 1918. (D3416)*

MacGregor, N.M., DSC

Mack, R.G. POW, *12th April 1917*

Mackay, W.W.

Macleod, K.D.

McLeod, J.S. (Equipment Officer)

McNeil, P.G.

Mayger, W.N. (Sgt Pilot) *Missing, 28th September 1918. (F3220)*

Malone, J. J., DSO *Killed in action, 30th April 1917*

Mather, A.S. POW, *1st May 1917*

Milne, C.G. POW, *20th September, 1918. (E4377)*

Morris, E.N.G. (Armament Officer)

Moyle, W.A. *Killed in mid-air collision over lines, 22nd March, 1918. (B7219)*

*Mulock, R.H., DSO, Legion d'Honneur

Murton, H.S. *Shot down and made POW, 4th May 1917*

Nelson, C.H. (Recording Officer)

Nelson, H. (Engineer Officer)

Nolan, T. *Injured accidentally, 1st September 1918. (D7162)*

Orchard, W.E. *Wounded in action and died 2nd June 1917*

Pickard, L.M.

Pierce, E.

Powell, L.A. *Wounded in action and died 6th April 1917*

Prideaux, E.R. *Missing, 17th May 1918. (B6408)*

Redpath, R.F.

Rochford, L.H. DSC, DFC

Rudge, A.E. *Killed in action, 22nd July 1918. (D9624)*

Sands, L.A. *Killed in mid-air collision over lines, 22nd March 1918. (B7216)*

Sehl, F.T.S.

Sidebottom, W., DFC

Skinner, H.W. *Wounded, 2nd October 1918. (D9638)*

Smith, S. *Killed in action, 11th April 1918. (B7277)*

Snow, A.C. (Armament Officer)

Stanton, E.

Stone, R.

Sutcliffe, C.W. *Injured accidentally, 31st July 1918. (D9594)*

Sutherland, H. (Sgt Pilot)

Sykes, R.

Taylor, A.G. (Sgt Pilot)

Taylor, F.D. (Recording Officer)

Towell, N. (Equipment Officer) *Wounded in raid, 31st July 1918*

Travers, H.G., DSC

Vernon, T.C.

Walker, W.R. *POW, 14th May 1917*

Walton, A.M.

Wambolt, H.R. *Killed in action 4th March 1917*
Webster, A.N. *Killed in action 5th June, 1918. (B7220)*
Whealy, A.T., DSC, DFC
White, J. P. *Killed in action 4th March 1917*
White, P.R. *POW, 16th May 1918. (D3353)*
Whiteley, R.I.
Wiggins, R.B.
Wigglesworth, H.E.P., DSC
Willy, C.M.
Wingfield, S.G.
Winter, P.R.
Wise, S.E.
Wood, P.
Woodhouse, D.H. *Injured accidentally, 31st August 1918. (E4374)*
Woodhouse, M.G.
Youens, H. St John. *POW, 23rd January 1918. (B7184)*

*denotes commanding officers of the squadron

APPENDIX 5

Aircraft flown by the author, 1916–19

Type	Serial Number
L & P Caudron (35 HP Anzani)	—
Maurice Farman 'Longhorn' (70 HP Renault)	8604, 146, 3010
Avro (80 HP Gnôme)	1046, 1002, 8596, 3314, 8585, 8591, 1028, 1047, 1048
Avro (100 Mono-Gnôme)	8599, 8577, 8977
Curtiss JN4	8824, 8859, 3425, 9, 8, 8853, 8857, 8863
BE2c (Curtiss engine)	4337
BE2c (90 RAF engine)	8623, 8620, 8615, 1164, 8495, 8405, 8610, 8624, 8408
Bristol Scout (80 Gnôme)	3016, 3034, 3042, 3014, 3052
Bristol Scout (100 Gnôme)	8978, 8970, 8972, 8965, 8973, 8989, 8969
Bristol Scout (80 Le Rhône)	3059
Pemberton-Billing Push-Proj (100 Mono-Gnôme)	9003
Nieuport (80 Le Rhône)	3967
Nieuport (110 Clerget)	8918
Sopwith 1½-strutter	9897
Sopwith Pup	N9900, N6161, N5197, N3691, N5199, N5196, N6170, N5194, N6207, N6465, N6461, N6209, N6181, N6460, N6162, N6209, N6467

Sopwith Camel (BR1)	B3807, N6364, B3783, B3857, B3786, B3796, B3940, B3798, B3808, N6377, B6241, B6257, B3865, B3858, B7189, B6401, B7203, B7222, B7197, D3353, B6408, D3371, D3344, D3413, D3414, D3855, D3417, D3403, B7185, D9618, D9633, D9583, D9585, D3376, C197, D9632, D9654, F3230, F3933, E4386, D9597
Sopwith Snipe	—
German DFW-Aviatik	—

Aircraft flown by the author,
1941–45

Type	Serial Number
Tiger Moth	K4258, T7112, R4778, T6517, T9811
Miles Magister	L8219, R1983, L8064, L8359, T9811,N3900
Proctor	P672, P6313, P6259, P6185, P6170, P6240, P6180, P6172, P6264, P6195, P6257, P6244, P6228, P6227, P6192, P6186, P5998, P6196, P6171, P6302, P6265, P6248, P6261, P6232, P6191, R7487, R7489, R7485, R7521, R7568, R7494, R7538, R7493, R7531, R7539, R7569, R7498, R7488, DX200, DX201, DX243, HM280, HM283, HM310, HM311, HM293, HM397, HM307, HM317, HM346, HM282, HM309, HM363, HM291, HM429, HM308, HM402, HM319, HM424, Z7197, Z7198, Z7203, Z7215, Z7194, Z7193, Z7220, Z7196, Z7202, Z7201, Z7237, Z7195, Z7199, Z7499, Z7238
Auster V	MT362
Hornet Moth	AW118

INDEX

(Contemporary Ranks)